Advance Praise for *Development in Latin America*

Maristella Svampa has been a lucid critical voice on Latin America's left turn in recent years and the continuation of an extractivist development model. She brings a rare combination of strong research and state of the art social theory. It is extremely welcome to see one of her key works translated into English. A must read for all interested in a progressive future for Latin America.
— Ronaldo Munck, author of *Rethinking Latin America: Development, Hegemony and Social Transformation.*

This book provides an holistic and multidisciplinary analysis of the dynamics of extractive capitalism in Latin America, its dire consequences and the forces of resistance. Svampa employs original and concise concepts to provide fresh insights into the contemporary dynamics of extractive capitalism in Latin America, its dire consequences and the forces of resistance.
— Darcy Tetreault, Estudios del Desarrollo, Universidad Autónoma de Zacatecas

D1055827

Development
in Latin America

ALSO IN THE CRITICAL DEVELOPMENT STUDIES SERIES

Politics Rules: Power, Globalization and Development (2019)
by Adam Sneyd

Critical Development Studies: An Introduction (2018)
by Henry Veltmeyer & Raúl Delgado Wise

Development
in Latin America:
Toward a New Future

MARISTELLA SVAMPA
TRANSLATION BY MARK RUSHTON

CRITICAL DEVELOPMENT STUDIES

FERNWOOD
PUBLISHING

Practical
ACTION
PUBLISHING

Editing: Erin Seatter
Design: John van der Woude, JVDW Designs
Printed and bound in Canada

Published in North America by Fernwood Publishing
32 Oceanvista Lane, Black Point, Nova Scotia, B0J 1B0
and 748 Broadway Avenue, Winnipeg, Manitoba, R3G 0X3
www.fernwoodpublishing.ca

Published in the rest of the world by Practical Action Publishing
27a Albert Street, Rugby, Warwickshire CV21 2SG, UK

Fernwood Publishing Company Limited gratefully acknowledges the financial support
of the Government of Canada through the Canada Book Fund and the Canada Council
for the Arts, the Nova Scotia Department of Communities, Culture and Heritage, the
Manitoba Department of Culture, Heritage and Tourism under the Manitoba
Publishers Marketing Assistance Program and the Province of Manitoba, through
the Book Publishing Tax Credit, for our publishing program.

Library and Archives Canada Cataloguing in Publication

Title: Development in Latin America: toward a new future / Maristella Svampa.
Names: Svampa, Maristella. author.
Description: Includes bibliographical references and index.
Identifiers: Canadiana 20190134615 | ISBN 9781773632162 (softcover)
Subjects: LCSH: Economic development—Latin America. | LCSH: Natural resources—
Latin America. |
LCSH: Capitalism—Latin America.
Classification: LCC HC125 .S83 2019 | DDC 338.98—dc23

Contents

Critical Development Studies Series

Three decades of uneven capitalist development and neoliberal globalization have devastated the economies, societies, livelihoods and lives of people around the world, especially those in societies of the Global South. Now more than ever, there is a need for a more critical, proactive approach to the study of global and development studies. The challenge of advancing and disseminating such an approach — to provide global and development studies with a critical edge — is on the agenda of scholars and activists from across Canada and the world and those who share the concern and interest in effecting progressive change for a better world.

This series provides a forum for the publication of small books in the interdisciplinary field of critical development studies — to generate knowledge and ideas about transformative change and alternative development. The editors of the series welcome the submission of original manuscripts that focus on issues of concern to the growing worldwide community of activist scholars in this field. Critical development studies (CDS) encompasses a broad array of issues ranging from the sustainability of the environment and livelihoods, the political economy and sociology of social inequality, alternative models of local and community-based development, the land and resource-grabbing dynamics of extractive capital, the subnational and global dynamics of political and economic power, and the forces of social change and resistance, as well as the contours of contemporary struggles against the destructive operations and ravages of capitalism and imperialism in the twenty-first century.

The books in the series are designed to be accessible to an activist readership as well as the academic community. The intent is to publish a series of small books (54,000 words, including bibliography, endnotes, index and front matter) on some of the biggest issues in the interdisciplinary field of critical development studies. To this end, activist scholars from across the world in the field of development studies and related academic disciplines are invited to submit a proposal or the draft of a book that conforms to the stated aim of the series. The editors will consider the submission of complete manuscripts within the 54,000-word limit. Potential authors are encouraged to submit a proposal that includes a rationale and short synopsis of the book, an outline of proposed chapters, one or two sample chapters, and a brief biography of the author(s).

Series Editors

HENRY VELTMEYER is a research professor at Universidad Autónoma de Zacatecas (Mexico) and professor emeritus of International Development Studies at Saint Mary's University (Canada), with a specialized interest in Latin American development. He is also co-chair of the Critical Development Studies Network and a co-editor of Fernwood's Agrarian Change and Peasant Studies series. The CDS Handbook: Tools for Change (Fernwood, 2011) was published in French by University of Ottawa Press as Des outils pour le changement : Une approche critique en études du développement and in Spanish as Herramientas para el Cambio, with funding from Oxfam UK by CIDES, Universidad Mayor de San Andrés, La Paz, Bolivia.

ANNETTE AURÉLIE DESMARAIS is the Canada Research Chair in Human Rights, Social Justice and Food Sovereignty at the University of Manitoba (Canada). She is the author of La Vía Campesina: Globalization and the Power of Peasants (Fernwood, 2007), which has been republished in French, Spanish, Korean, Italian and Portuguese, and Frontline Farmers: How the National Farmers Union Resists Agribusiness and Creates our New Food Future (Fernwood, 2019). She is co-editor of Food Sovereignty: Reconnecting Food, Nature and Community (Fernwood, 2010); Food Sovereignty in Canada: Creating Just and Sustainable Food Systems (Fernwood, 2011); and Public Policies for Food Sovereignty: Social Movements and the State (Routledge, 2017).

RAÚL DELGADO WISE is a research professor and director of the PhD program in Development Studies at the Universidad Autónoma de Zacatecas (Mexico). He holds the prestigious UNESCO Chair on Migration and Development and is executive director of the International Migration and Development Network, as well as author and editor of some twenty books and more than a hundred essays. He is a member of the Mexican Academy of Sciences and editor of the book series, Latin America and the New World Order, for Miguel Angel Porrúa publishers and chief editor of the journal Migración y Desarrollo. He is also a member of the international working group, People's Global Action on Migration Development and Human Rights.

Introduction

A
t the beginning of the twenty-first century, Latin American economies greatly benefited from the high international prices of primary
products (commodities) and began a period of economic growth.
This juncture coincided with a new period characterized by the questioning and widespread rejection of the neoliberal consensus and traditional
forms of political representation, as well as intense social mobilizations.
Subsequently, in various countries of the region, a cycle of protest against
the neoliberal agenda was crowned by the emergence of left and centre-left
governments with "progressive" policy agendas that combined heterodox
economic policies — the use of revenues derived from the export of commodities to finance social programs oriented towards poverty reduction.
Thus began the so-called Latin American progressive cycle, which would
extend from the turn of the new millennium until 2015–16.

During this period of extraordinary profitability, Latin American governments over and above ideological differences tended to underline the
comparative advantages of the commodities boom, denying or minimizing
the new economic, social, environmental and territorial inequalities and
asymmetries brought about by an extractive model of capitalist development — the large-scale exportation of raw materials (minerals, metals, oil
and gas, agri-food products). Over the course of the commodities boom
on the world market, governments in the region virtually without exception enabled a turn back towards a productivist vision of development
and sought to deny or distract from discussions about the development
implications (impacts, consequences, damages) of the export extractive
model. Moreover, they deliberately ramped up mega-dam and mining
ventures (open-pit mines) while expanding the extractive frontier in the
countryside — the latter through agro-monocultures such as soybeans,
biofuels and oil palms.

Gradually and before the outbreak and spread of conflict on the extractive frontier, a concept with diverse analytical dimensions and mobilizing power began to travel through the region to characterize the emerging phenomenon: *neoextractivism*. It is true that this was not a completely new development, because its origins go back to the conquest and colonization of Latin America by Europe at the dawn of capitalism. However, at the turn of the new century, the phenomenon of extractivism acquired new dimensions, not only in objective terms in regard to the quantity and scale of extractive projects, the different types of activity and the national and transnational actors involved, but also subjectively in terms of the emergence of new forces of social resistance, which questioned the advance of the commodity frontier and developed other narratives against dispossession and in defence of values such as land, territory, the commons and nature.

At the same time, the conflicts generated by the new dynamics of capital accumulation resulted in confrontations between, on the one hand, peasant-Indigenous organizations, socioterritorial movements and environmental groups and, on the other hand, governments and multinational corporations in the extractive sector, including not only conservative and neoliberal regimes but also the progressive postneoliberal regimes on the centre-left that had awakened so many political expectations. Defined as neoextractivism, the new phase of capitalist development has introduced dilemmas and fractures within the field of mobilized social organizations and the Left, fractures that show the limits of the progressivism that exists, as seen in its link to neoliberal authoritarianism and hegemonic political and development practice. Far from signifying a weakening of extractivism, the end of the commodities supercycle in 2013 confronted us with a deepening of the phenomenon as a strategy of economic development across the region. At present, the equation "the more extractivism, the less democracy" is illustrated by the loosening of existing environmental regulatory regimes, as well as the deepening of social disorganization and criminalization and an increase in the murders of environmental activists within the context of disputes over land, territory and access to the commons.

In this book I examine the advance of capital on the extractive frontier in Latin America. The first chapter presents some of the critical concepts related to this problem. These include neoextractivism, the Commodities Consensus and the developmentalist illusion. I give an account of how these concepts shed light on the current crisis of capitalist development and neoextractivism in its various dimensions. In Chapter 2, I discuss different levels of the socioenvironmental conflict associated with extractivism, as well as the new discourse of territorial valuation emerging in light of these struggles — what I have called the ecoterritorial turn. In Chapter 3, I propose an approach to the complexities presented by the current ecoterritorial turn, which I see as a feature of existing socioenvironmental struggles, emphasizing the dilemmas that relate to recognition of and respect for Indigenous rights, as well as the expansion of new forms of popular feminism. In Chapter 4, I provide an account of the trends associated with the new phase of neoextractivism: criminal territorialities, state and parastatal violence and patriarchal violence, along with the expansion of what I refer to as extreme energy, which involves newer methods of fossil fuel extraction using advanced technologies (e.g., fracking, deep water drilling, oil sands processing) to access increasingly difficult-to-reach resources. Chapter 5 explores the geopolitical context of capitalist development on the extractive frontier, and the forms of the new dependency developed in relation to China. It also explores the limits of the progressive cycle and proposes a balanced assessment that includes but goes beyond the expansion of neoextractive capitalism in the region.

The book closes with a reflection on the systemic crisis. Here I take up the concept of the Anthropocene in a diagnosis that links the global socioecological crisis with a critique of current development models. I also explore some concepts that traverse both critical development studies and the counterhegemonic language of social movements in Latin America and Europe.

NOTE

This book was originally written in Spanish and has been translated by Mark Rushton.

1 Neoextractivism and Development

I n this first chapter I present the key concepts that inform the critical perspective and analysis throughout this book — namely, neoextractivism, the Commodities Consensus and the developmentalist illusion. In addition, I establish several lines of continuity and rupture between the concepts of extractivism and neoextractivism.

Extractivism and Neoextractivism

Invented in Latin America, neoextractivism is a productive analytical category that has a great descriptive and explanatory power, as well as a denunciatory character and strong mobilizing capability. It appears both as an analytical category and as a powerful political concept, because it speaks eloquently about power relations and disputes at play, and it also refers, beyond currently existing asymmetries, to a set of shared but also differentiated responsibilities between the Global North and South, between the centre and its peripheries. Insofar as it alludes to unsustainable development patterns and warns of the deepening logic of dispossession, it has the particularity of illuminating a set of multiscale problems that define different dimensions of the current crisis.

It is impossible to fully synthesize the complex literature on neoextractivism due to the profusion of articles and books on the subject, which includes works on the use that those directly impacted by the advance of extractive capital — the communities and social movements on the extractive frontier — have made and are making of the category of neoextractivism. But in this first approximation I am interested in giving an account of some readings that point to the multidimensionality and multiscalarity of the phenomenon. Thus, for example, all of the authors in this field of study recognize the historical roots of extractivism as a mode of accumulation. In the view of Ecuadorian economist Alberto Acosta, "extractivism is a form of accumulation ... forged some 500 years ago" and determined since then by the demands of the metropolitan centres of nascent capitalism (Acosta 2013). Along this line, Argentinian sociologist Horacio Machado Aráoz affirms that extractivism is not just another phase of capitalism, or a problem of certain underdeveloped economies on the periphery of the system, but rather "a structural feature of capitalism as a world system," a "historical-geopolitical product of the original differentiation-hierarchization of colonial territories and imperial metrópoli, the former regarded as mere spaces for the looting and plundering for the supply of the others" (Machado Aráoz 2013). Likewise, Venezuelan sociologist Emiliano Terán Mantovani argues that neoextractivism can be read as a particular "mode of accumulation," especially in regard to Latin American economies that "can be studied from the social and territorial scope encompassed by the nation-state without detriment to other scales of territorial analysis" (Terán Mantovani 2016).

Other outstanding works on this question consider extractivism as a form of development based on the extraction and appropriation of natural resources, which feeds a scarcely diversified productive framework that is very dependent on an international division of labour in which the peripheral economies on the frontier of extractive capital serve as suppliers of raw materials. Thus, for Uruguayan environmental thinker Eduardo Gudynas, extractivism refers to a "mode of appropriation" rather than a mode of production; it is "a type of extraction of natural resources" that refers to activities that extract large volumes of natural resources in unprocessed or relatively unprocessed (primary) form for the purpose of meeting the demand for these resources on the world market — and for appropriating the surplus value and resource rents generated in the process. Throughout history, there have been successive generations of extractivism, the most recent of which is characterized not so much by the extraction of minerals and metals and the exploitation of agricultural labour as by the appropriation and intensive use of water, energy and resources. Also, there are differences between traditional extractivism as practised by the most conservative or neoliberal governments in the region and "progressive neoextractivism," where the state plays a more active role in capturing a part of the surplus as a source of additional fiscal revenues that can be directed towards the reduction of poverty.

Although progressive extractivism, or neoextractivism, has acquired a social legitimacy denied to the extractivism practised by the remaining or returning neoliberal regimes in the region, it has not escaped the exceedingly sharp contradictions of extractive capitalism; the negative social and environmental impacts of extractive capital and its destructive operations have been reproduced in the most progressive extractive regimes, such as Ecuador under the presidency of Rafael Correa (Gudynas 2009, 2015).

My own particular perspective coincides with much of this analysis. The historical-structural dimension of extractivism is linked to the invention of Europe and the advance of capital in the development process — the expansion of capitalism as a world system. Associated with a history of conquest and genocide, extractivism in Latin America has a long history. Since the arrival of the conquistadors in the sixteenth century, Latin America has been the preserve of imperialist exploitation, destruction and looting. Rich in natural resources, the region was reconfigured again and again in successive economic cycles, imposed by the logic of capital through the expansion of the extractive frontier — reconfigurations that at a local level led to great contrasts between extraordinary profitability and extreme poverty, as well as a great loss of human lives and the degradation and despoliation of territories converted into areas of sacrifice. For example, Potosí, Bolivia, marked the birth of a particular large-scale appropriation of nature and of a mode of accumulation characterized by the export of raw materials from the periphery of the system and its subordinate position in the world economy. Internal specialization and external dependence consolidated what the Venezuelan anthropologist Fernando Coronil has aptly termed "nature-exporting societies."

However, the history of extractivism in the region is not linear; it is traversed by successive economic cycles dependent on the demands of the world market, as well as by the consolidation processes of the nation-state, especially in the middle of the twentieth century, which allowed a certain control over extraordinary incomes and revenues generated by the capitalist development of both mining and oil, the intensive exploitation of both labour and nature.

At the beginning of the twenty-first century, extractivism was loaded with new dimensions. In this context, where it is possible to register continuities and ruptures, the concept of extractivism reappeared as neoextractivism. Continuities are seen because, during successive economic cycles, the extractivist DNA with which European capital marked the region's long-term memory was also feeding a certain social conception about nature and its benefits. As a result, extractivism was associated not only with dispossession and the large-scale looting of natural resources but also with the comparative advantages and economic opportunities that emerged at the same time as the different economic cycles and the new role of an interventionist state. Not by chance, neoextractivism, faced with the prevailing progressive governments, reinvigorated the developmentalist illusion expressed in the idea that, thanks to the opportunities offered by the new commodities boom and even more by the active role of the state, it would be possible to achieve development.

Ruptures are seen because the new phase of capital accumulation, characterized by the strong pressure put on natural goods and territories, and even more by the dizzying expansion of the commodities frontier, opened up new political, social and ecological disputes and social resistance against the dominant developmentalist imaginary. New forms of collective action questioned the developmentalist illusion while denouncing the consolidation of a single-commodity model that destroys biodiversity and entails land-grabbing, the destruction of pre-existing forces of development and the degradation of both the environment and territories used for production and sustainable rural livelihoods.

Neoextractivism as a "Privileged Window" on Capitalist Development in the Region

In order to grasp the specificity of contemporary neoextractivism, I propose a reading of it at two levels: first, a general reading in which neoextractivism emerges as a "privileged window" that allows for an account of the major dimensions of the current global crisis, and second, a more specific reading in which neoextractivism appears as a sociopolitical-territorial model for understanding the dynamics of local and regional development. Far from being a flat category, neoextractivism, in the form it has assumed over the last fifteen years in Latin America, constitutes a complex concept that provides a privileged window for viewing the complexities and different levels of the multifaceted crisis that contemporary societies are experiencing.

First, neoextractivism is at the centre of diverse contemporary accumulation dynamics. Indeed, as several authors have pointed out, the increase of the social metabolism of capital within the framework of advanced capitalism demands for its maintenance an ever-increasing quantity of raw materials and energy, which translates into greater pressure on natural resources and territories. Although the metabolic exchange between humans and nature is dealt with only marginally in the writings of Marx,[1] it has been studied systematically by several representatives of critical (and ecological) Marxism in more recent times. Both O'Connor (2001) and Foster (2000) emphasize the costs of the natural elements involved in the advance of both constant and variable capital, as well as land and resource rents and negative externalities of all kinds. While Foster talks about "the metabolic fracture," O'Connor calls this process "the second contradiction of capitalism," noting that "there is no single term that has the same theoretical interpretation as the rate of exploitation in the first contradiction" (capital/labour). Likewise, both authors highlight the appropriation and self-destructive use by capital of the labour force, infrastructure, urban space and nature or the environment.[2]

A complementary reading of the so-called "second contradiction of capitalism" is offered by geographer David Harvey (2003), who places the process of primitive accumulation of capital, analyzed by Marx in *Capital* — that is, the expropriation and dispossession of the land from the peasantry, who are thrown into the labour market as proletarians — at the centre of the development process. In terms of the concept of "accumulation by dispossession," often cited in the Latin American literature, this updated interpretation highlights the importance of the dynamic of dispossession in the current expansion and advance of capital on goods, people and territories. This reading recognizes an important precedent in the work of Rosa Luxemburg, who at the beginning of the twentieth century observed the continuous character of "original, or primitive, accumulation," rather than associating it, as Marx did, exclusively with the origins of capitalism.

Second, neoextractivism illuminates the crisis of the project of modernity, and more generally the current socioecological crisis. Certainly, the imminence that we are witnessing of major anthropogenic and sociogenic changes on a planetary scale that endanger life (the Anthropocene) has led to a questioning of the current dynamics of development linked to unlimited expansion of the commercialization frontier, as well as the dualist vision associated with modernity. Consequently, it is possible to establish a relationship between neoextractivism (as a dynamic of dominant development) and the Anthropocene (as a critique of a specific model of modernity) when examining its consequences globally. The ecological crisis thus appears intrinsically linked to the crisis of modernity. Arturo Escobar (2005) in this regard urges us to think of alternatives to modernity, other paradigms that place the reproduction of life at the centre of analysis and point to the need to view and re-create the link between humans and non-humans from a critical non-dualistic perspective.

Third, neoextractivism also connects us with the global economic crisis insofar as the current model of accumulation is associated with the reforms carried out by neoliberal and financial capitalism from the 1990s onward as well as the propensity towards crisis reflected in the global financial crisis of 2008. On the one hand, financial capital plays a fundamental role in the extraction of raw materials, in the organization of the logistics of their circulation (Gago and Mezzadra 2017) and of course in determining increases and decreases in the prices of commodities in international markets. On the other hand, the crisis has accentuated social inequalities, based on an economic adjustment policy to combat the recession that extended to the central countries and made economic models that more intensely commodify nature attractive. In this way, the so-called green economy model based on inclusion (inclusive growth and sustainable development) is being promoted from a mainstream development perspective. This model extends the financial format of the carbon market to other elements of nature, such as air, water and processes and functions of the environment (Svampa and Viale 2014).

Fourth, neoextractivism provides a privileged window that allows us to read the development of capital(ism) in geopolitical terms, from the relative decline of the US and the rise of China as a global power. This situation of hegemonic transition is interpreted as entry into a period characterized by conflicting polycentrism and plurality in cultural-civilizational terms, the consequences of which are still to be defined. From the globalized peripheries, in Latin America, Africa and certain regions of Asia, the hegemonic transition brought as a correlate the intensification of exports of raw materials, which is reflected in the consolidation of increasingly unequal economic and socioecological links to economies at the centre and especially the Republic of China. In other words, in the current geopolitical context, which points to the great Asian country as a new global power, neoextractivism allows us to read the process of global reconfiguration, which from the perspective of peripheral capitalism implicates the expansion of the extractive frontier and a dizzying refocusing of economies on the periphery on the production of primary products.

Last but not least, neoextractivism provides a privileged window for reading the development process in terms of the crisis of democracy — that is, the relationship between political regime, democracy and respect for human rights. Certainly, the association between neoextractivism and the weakening of democracy is indisputable: without social licence, without consultation of the population, without environmental controls and with the scarce presence of the state, or even with it, the trend is towards the manipulation of forms of popular participation in order to control collective decision-making. On the other hand, the increase in state and parastatal violence raises a question about the always tense links between extractivism and human rights. Given the growing criminalization of socioenvironmental protests and the increasing murders of environmental activists throughout the world, particularly in Latin America, the perverse equation "more extractivism, less democracy" (Svampa 2016) points to a dangerous slip towards political closure.

In short, extractivism is part of the long history of the continent and its struggles, and it defines an appropriation of nature and a pattern of colonial accumulation associated with the birth of modern capitalism. However, in its updated form in the twenty-first century, it brings new dimensions at different levels: global (hegemonic transition, expansion of the commodity frontier, depletion of non-renewable natural resources, socioecological crisis of planetary scope), regional and national (relationship between the extractive-export model, the nation-state and the capture of extraordinary income), territorial (intensive occupation of land, ecoterritorial struggles with the participation of different collective actors) and lastly policies (emergence of a new, contentious political grammar, increase in state and parastatal violence).

Neoextractivism as Development and a Socioterritorial Model

Contemporary neoextractivism can be characterized as a development model based on the overexploitation of increasingly scarce, largely non-renewable natural goods, as well as the expansion of exploitation into territories previously considered unproductive from the point of view of capital. It is characterized by its orientation towards the large-scale export of primary goods, including hydrocarbons (gas and oil), metals and minerals (copper, gold, silver, tin, bauxite and zinc, among others) and products linked to the new agrarian paradigm (soybean, oil palms, sugar cane). Defined in this way, neoextractivism designates something more than the activities traditionally considered as extractive, since it includes open-pit mega-mining, the expansion of the oil and energy frontier and the construction of large hydroelectric dams and other infrastructure works (waterways, ports, bi-oceanic corridors and more), as well as the expansion of different forms of monocultures or single-commodity production through the generalization of the agribusiness model and the overexploitation of fisheries or forest monocultures.

In this vein, neoextractivism is also a useful sociopolitical-territorial model for analysis of development and resistance dynamics at national, regional or local levels. For example, the expansion of the soybean frontier led to a reconfiguration of the rural world in several South American countries. From 2000 to 2014 alone, soybean plantations in South America expanded by 29 million hectares, comparable to the size of Ecuador. Brazil and Argentina account for close to 90 percent of regional production, although the fastest expansion has occurred in Uruguay, and Paraguay is the country where soybean occupies the largest area relative to other crops at 75 percent of total agricultural production (Oxfam 2016: 30).

Another major feature of neoextractivism is the large scale of the ventures, which also tells us about the size of the investments, since these are capital-intensive, rather than work-intensive, projects. This refers to the character of the intervening actors — in general, large transnational corporations — although of course the so-called trans-Latins are not excluded — that is, national mega-companies such as Petróleo Brasileiro (Petrobras), Petróleos de Venezuela and even Argentina's Yacimientos Petrolíferos Fiscales, among others. At the same time, this warns us about an important variable of megaprojects: they generate few jobs directly (and reach the maximum in the construction stage of the enterprise). For example, in the case of large-scale mining, for every million dollars invested, only 0.5 to 2 direct jobs are created (Colectivo Voces de Alerta 2011). In Peru, a country par excellence of transnational mega-mining, it occupies barely 2 percent of the economically active population, against 23 percent in agriculture, 16 percent in commerce and almost 10 percent in manufacturing (Lang and Mokrani 2013).

Likewise, neoextractivism presents a certain territorial dynamic whose tendency is the intensive occupation of territory and land-grabbing, through forms linked to monoculture or single-commodity production, one of whose consequences is the displacement of other forms of production (local and regional economies) as well as populations. In this way, at the beginning of the twenty-first century, neoextractivism redefined the dispute over land, which unevenly pits poor and vulnerable populations against major economic players interested in implementing transgenic crops linked to soybeans, oil palms, sugar cane and others. According to a 2016 Oxfam report using data from the agricultural censuses of fifteen countries in Latin America, 1 percent of the larger farms concentrate more than half of the agricultural area; "in other words, one percent of farms occupy more land than the remaining 99 percent." Colombia is the most unequal in regard to distribution of land, as 0.4 percent of agricultural holdings dominate 68 percent of the country's land. The top 1 percent of farms also dominate the land in Peru (77 percent), Chile (74 percent), Paraguay (71 percent), Bolivia (66 percent), Mexico (56 percent), Brazil (44 percent) and Argentina (36 percent).[3]

According to Gian Carlo Delgado, the concentration of land results from the dynamics of accumulation by dispossession — the appropriation of land for one or more the following purposes:

1. monoculture, including the so-called wild or flex crops, such as the food/bioenergy/production inputs of corn, sugar cane and oil palms as well as non-food inputs such as cellulose;
2. access, management and usufruct of resources, such as energy and non-energy minerals;
3. access to water (or blue grabbing); and
4. conservation, or the so-called green appropriation of land or green grabbing, which ranges from the creation of private protected areas to the establishment of climate change mitigation projects such as the so-called redd+ (reduce emissions from deforestation and degradation + conservation) projects (Delgado 2016).

The Commodities Consensus and the Developmentalist Illusion

In Latin America, neoextractivism expanded in a period of change marked by the move away from the Washington Consensus, associated with financial valorization and structural adjustment, and into what I call the Commodities Consensus, based on the large-scale exportation of primary goods, economic growth and the expansion of consumption capacity (Svampa 2013). Indeed, unlike in the 1990s, Latin American economies as of 2000–03 were favoured by the high international prices of primary products (commodities), which was reflected in trade balances and fiscal surpluses. This fact cannot be dismissed, especially after the long period of stagnation and economic regression of the previous decades, particularly the openly neoliberal period of the nineties. In this favourable economic climate — at least until 2013 — Latin American governments tended to emphasize the comparative advantages of the commodities boom while denying or minimizing the new inequalities and socioenvironmental asymmetries, which brought the consolidation of a development model based on the large-scale export of raw materials. In this way, all Latin American governments, regardless of ideology, enabled the return of a productivist vision of development, which, together with the developmentalist illusion, led to the denial and avoidance of substantive discussions about the social, environmental, territorial and political impacts of neoextractivism, as well as the diminishing of emerging socioenvironmental mobilizations and protests.

As for the matter of consequences, the Commodities Consensus was characterized by a complex, vertiginous and recursive dynamic, which must be read from a variety of angles. From an economic point of view, it translated into a return to a primary economy, visible in the reorientation towards primary extractive activities, with little added value. This effect was aggravated by the ascension of China as a global economic power oriented towards the extraction and importation of natural resources to meet domestic demand for industrial inputs and consumer goods.

Latin American exports to China, as well as Chinese investment in the region, have been much more concentrated in primary commodities — especially extractive commodities — than Latin American economic relations with the rest of the world. In 2014, in the Mercosur countries, exports of primary goods as a percentage of total exports ranged from 65 percent in Brazil to 90 percent in Paraguay (CEPAL 2015).[4] For this reason, even a country like Brazil, which has a diversified economy, suffered what French economist Pierre Salama (2011) characterized as a phenomenon of "early deindustrialization."

The Commodities Consensus can be read both in terms of ruptures and continuities in relation to the previous period of the Washington Consensus. Ruptures are seen because there are important elements of differentiation with respect to the nineties, which are associated with the Washington Consensus, whose agenda was based on a policy of adjustments, privatizations and financial valorization, which ended up redefining the state as an all-powerful regulatory agent. Likewise, neoliberalism brought a kind of political homogenization to the region, marked by adherence to World Bank prescriptions. In contrast, the Commodities Consensus put export-oriented extractive projects at the centre, establishing a space of greater flexibility and activism regarding the role of the state, but also allowing for the coexistence of progressive governments that seriously question the orthodox version of the neoliberal consensus and those governments that continue to deepen a conservative political matrix within the institutional framework of the neoliberal policy agenda.

Certainly, from a progressive perspective, the Commodities Consensus is associated with the agency and activism of the state, as well as a battery of economic and social policies — whose base was the extraordinary income associated with the extractive-export model — directed to the most vulnerable sectors. In the new context, certain tools and institutional capacities of the state were recovered, and the state once again became a regulatory actor and, in some cases, a redistributive agent. However, within the framework of the theories of world governance, which point to an institutional framework based on supranational frameworks, the tendency is not precisely for the national state to become a mega-actor or for its intervention to guarantee fundamental changes. On the contrary, the most likely scenario is the return of a moderately regulating state capable of settling in a space of variable geometry — that is, in a multisectoral scheme with the complexity of civil society, illustrated by social movements, nongovernmental organizations (NGOS) and other actors, but in close association with multinational capital, whose weight in Latin American economies, far from retreating, has increased significantly. Thus, although the progressive approach has been unorthodox and has departed from neoliberalism in terms of the guiding role of the state, as noted by Argentinian economist Mariano Féliz, it was far from questioning the hegemony of transnational capital in the peripheral economy (Féliz 2012: 24–27). This reality placed clear limits on the actions of the national state as well as on the demands for democratization of collective decisions coming from the communities and populations affected by the large extractive projects.

On the other hand, a large part of the Left and populist progressivism in Latin America continue to hold a productivist vision of development,[5] which is nourished by a tendency to read social conflict in terms of opposition between capital and labour, minimizing or paying scant attention to capital-nature relations, even in the new social struggles concentrated in the defence of territory and the commons. In this context, especially at the beginning of the progressive cycle, the dynamics of dispossession tended to become a blind, non-conceptualizable point. As a consequence, socioenvironmental problems were considered a secondary concern relative to structural problems of poverty and exclusion. Thus, in spite of the fact that in the last decades the Latin American Left and populism carried out a process of revalorization of the community-Indigenous matrix, a large part continues to adhere to a productivist and efficiency vision of development, closely linked to a hegemonic ideology of progress based on confidence in the expansion of the productive forces.

Consequently, the progressive governments sought to justify neo-extractivism as a way to generate foreign currency for the state — then reoriented to the redistribution of income and domestic consumption — or activities with higher added value. This discourse, whose real scope should be analyzed case by case and according to different phases or moments, sought to simplistically play the social question (redistribution, social policies) against the environmental problem (the preservation of the commons, the conservation and protection of land), while leaving out complex and fundamental discussions on development, environmental sustainability and democracy. In fact, in the name of "comparative advantages," Latin American governments sought to promote a model of inclusion associated with consumption, using a plebeian-progressive discourse and even denying its short-term nature. This transitory link between state advancement, economic growth and a consumer-citizen model made possible the continued electoral success and power of the different governments.

The confirmation of Latin America as an adaptive economy with respect to the different cycles of accumulation, and therefore acceptance of the place it occupies in the global division of labour, constitutes one of the core elements that underpin the Washington Consensus and the Commodities Consensus. Beyond this, the progressive governments have emphasized a rhetoric of economic autonomy and national sovereignty, and talked about the construction of a Latin American space.

Finally, the development model was not only supported by an instrumentalist and productivist vision, it was also based upon a revised conceptualization of the historical abundance of natural resources (the continent's El Dorado vision). In some countries, this imaginary appeared connected with the experience of the crisis — that is, with the exclusionary legacy of the nineties, which increased inequality and poverty. For example, the end of "the long neoliberal night," in the words of former Ecuadorian president Rafael Correa, had a political and economic correlate, linked to the great crisis of the first years of the twenty-first century (which saw unemployment, a reduction of opportunities, migration and political instability). This topic also recurrently appears in the speeches of former Argentinian presidents Néstor and Cristina Fernández de Kirchner, in regards to conditions of economic growth under their governments that represented a notable recovery from the legacy of economic crisis left by the neoliberal regime of Carlos Menem in the 1990s, a legacy that ended with the great crisis that shook that country in 2001–02, a cycle of progressive reforms and the search for a new model oriented towards neodevelopmentalism (inclusive development in the form of poverty reduction).

Thus, within a post–Washington Consensus framework on the need for the state to become more actively involved in the development process, and during the advance of capital on the extractive frontier, Latin America resumed the foundational myth of progressive development — what I have called the developmentalist illusion — expressed in the idea that thanks to economic opportunities provided by the primary commodities boom (rising raw material prices and growing demand, mainly from China), it would be possible to quickly close the gap between the region and the industrialized countries, in order to reach that always promised but never realized development of Latin American societies. Whether in the discourse of dispossession (the liberal perspective) or state control over surplus (progressive perspective), current development models based on an extractivist paradigm re-evoked the El Dorado imaginary that runs throughout the history of the continent.

Consequently, the Latin American scenario demonstrated not only a convergence between neoextractivism, the developmentalist illusion and neoliberalism, as seen paradigmatically in the cases of Peru, Colombia and Mexico, but also between neoextractivism, the developmentalist illusion and progressive governments, which complicated the relationship between Indigenous and socioenvironmental movements. The most paradoxical situations in Latin American during the Commodities Consensus and the apogee of the progressive cycle were found in Bolivia and Ecuador. This is not a minor issue, given that it was in these countries, within the framework of participatory processes, where new concepts such as the plurinational state, autonomous regions, *buen vivir* (living well, in social solidarity and harmony with nature) and the rights of nature were born and then reflected in the construction of new constitutions that established the formation of a multiethnic and plurinational state. However, with the consolidation of these progressive regimes, other issues, linked to the export of raw materials and their relationship with economic growth, began to assume importance.

As I understand it, the Commodities Consensus also has a political-ideological charge, because it alludes to a tacit or explicit agreement about the irresistible nature of the current extractivist dynamics, a product of the growing global demand for primary goods. As in the 1980s and '90s — the golden years of neoliberalism, when the dominant discourse affirmed there was no alternative — from 2000 onward the political elites of the region (both progressive and conservative) argued there was no alternative to extractivism, aiming thereby to constrain or dampen collective resistance on the basis of the "common sense" and "reasonableness" of different versions of progressive capitalism while establishing a new limit with respect to the production of alternatives. As Mirta Antonelli argues, the imposition of a single narrative and with it a single possible world seeks to control and neutralize logics that sustain other arguments, other reasonings, other memories and feelings, other societal projects (Antonelli 2011: 11).

Consequently, critical discourse or radical opposition is categorized as irrationality, antimodernity and a denial of progress and the rights of nature (Pachamamism), and alleged to be driven by particular NGOs or foreign agents. So, unlike the 1990s, when the continent appeared to be under the sway of the neoliberal model, which was viewed as the only way forward — there is no alternative, Margaret Thatcher was famously or infamously reported to have declared —the new century has been marked by a set of tensions and contradictions that are difficult to process. The passage from the Washington Consensus to the Commodities Consensus has meant new problems and paradoxes that have reconfigured the horizons of Latin American critical thinking. The rest of this book attempts to reconstruct this field of critical development studies.

NOTES

1. Michael Lowy (2011) points out in his writings that this critical perspective linked to a metabolic exchange between the human being and nature (which gives rise to the ecological crisis) is dissociated from the productivist side of Marxism predominant in the twentieth century. See Sacher (2016) and also Delgado (2016).
2. In this vein, already in the 1970s, Marxist authors such as Henri Lefebvre stressed the need to expand our readings on the dynamics of capital. Thus, in the face of the "ossified dialectic of capital and labour" (quoted in Coronil 2002), the French sociologist made an appeal to a dialectic of capital, labour and land, not only referring to the powers of nature but also the agents associated with it, including the state, which exercises sovereignty over a national territory.
3. The Oxfam data refer to farms and not to people. Therefore, the data do not count landless peasants and provide very little information about collective property (for the cases of Bolivia, Colombia and Peru).
4. According to Burchardt, it is necessary to distinguish three regional dynamics in the context of expansion of extractive economies in Latin America. On the one hand, there are those countries, such as Ecuador and Venezuela (oil), Peru and Chile (mining) and Bolivia (gas), that stand out for their reliance on single-commodity production through the export of raw materials. Then there are those countries that have a diversified economy but have effectively increased their extractive sectors, as is the case of Brazil with mining, soy and now oil through the pre-salt oil reserves. Finally, there are the countries of Central America and Mexico, which during the first phase of the Commodities Consensus had not fully committed to extractivism, though they are clearly moving in that direction (Burchardt 2016: 63).
5. Productivism is based on the idea of indefinite growth and implies a non-recognition of the planet's sustainability limits. An excellent definition is provided by Joaquim Sampere, who uses the term "productivism" to designate any social metabolism that does not respect the limits of ecological sustainability because it believes that the human species can afford to exploit at will and without regard to the limits of natural resources (Sampere 2015).

REFERENCES

Acosta, Alberto. 2013. "Extractivism and Neoextractivism: Two Sides of the Same Curse." In M. Lang and D. Mokrani (eds.), *Beyond Development: Alternative Visions from Latin America*. Amsterdam, The Netherlands, Transnational Institute and Rosa Luxembourg Foundation.

Antonelli, Mirta. 2011. "Megaminería, desterritorialización del Estado y biopolítica."

Astrolabio 7. <https://revistas.unc.edu.ar/index.php/astrolabio/article/viewFile/592/3171>.

Burchardt, Hans-Jürgen. 2016. "El neo-extractivismo en el siglo xxi: Qué podemos aprender del ciclo de desarrollo más reciente en América Latina." In Has-Jürgen Burchardt, Rafael Domínguez, Carlos Larrea and Stefan Peters (eds.), *Nada dura para siempre. Neoextractivismo despúes del boom de las materias primas*. Ecuador: Abya Yala.

CEPAL. 2015. *Anuario Estadístico de América Latina y el Caribe*. Santiago de Chile: CEPAL.

Colectivo Voces de Alerta. 2011. *15 mitos y realidades sobre la minería transnacional en Argentina*. Buenos Aires: Editorial El Colectivo-Ediciones Herramienta.

Coronil, Fernando. 2002. *El Estado mágico. Naturaleza, dinero y modernidad en Venezuela*. Venezuela: Consejo de Desarrollo Científico y Humanístico de la Universidad Central de Venezuela-Nueva Sociedad.

Delgado, Gian Carlo. 2016. "Configuraciones del territorio: Despojo, transiciones y alternativas." In Navarro Mina and Daniele Fini (eds.), *Despojo capitalista y luchas comunitarias en defensa de la vida en México, Claves desde la Ecología Política*. México: Universidad Benemérita de Puebla.

Escobar, A. 2005. "El post-desarrollo como concepto y práctica social." In D. Mato (ed.), *Políticas de Economía, ambiente y sociedad en tiempos de globalización*. Caracas: Facultad de Ciencias Económicas y Sociales, Universidad Central de Venezuela.

Féliz, Mariano. 2012. "Proyecto sin clase: Crítica al neoestructuralismo como fundamento del neodesarrollismo." En Mariano Féliz et al. (eds.), *Más allá del individuo. Clases sociales, transformaciones económicas y políticas estatales en la Argentina contemporánea*. Buenos Aires: El Colectivo.

Foster, John Bellamy. 2000. *La Ecología de Marx: materialismo y naturaleza*. España: El Viejo Topo.

Gago, Verónica, and Sandro Mezzadra. 2017. "A Critique of the Extractive Operations of Capital: Toward an Expanded Concept of Extractivism." *Rethinking Marxism*, 29, 4: 574–591.

Gudynas, Eduardo. 2009. "La ecología política del giro biocéntrico en la nueva Constitución del Ecuador." *Revista de Estudios Sociales*, 32: 34–47.

Gudynas, Eduardo. 2015. *Extractivismos. Ecología, economía y política de un modo de entender el desarrollo y la naturaleza*. Bolivia: Claes- CEDIB.

Harvey, David. 2003. *The New Imperialism*. New York: Oxford University Press.

Lang, Miriam, and Dunia Mokrani (eds.). 2013. *Beyond Development: Alternative Visions from Latin America*. Amsterdam, The Netherlands: Transnational Institute and Rosa Luxembourg Foundation.

Lowy, Michael. 2011. *Ecosocialismo. La alternativa radical a la catástrofe ecológica capitalista*. Buenos Aires: Editorial El Colectivo-Ediciones Herramienta.

Machado Aráoz, Horacio. 2013. "Crisis ecológica, conflictos socioambientales y orden neocolonial. Las paradojas de Nuestra América en las fronteras del extractivismo." *Revista Brasileira de Estudos Latino-Americanos*, 3, 1: 118–155. <http://rebela.edugraf.ufsc.br/index.php/pc/article/ view/137>.

O'Connor, James. 2001. "Causas naturales. Ensayo de marxismo ecológico."

Buenos Aires: Siglo xxi. <http://theomai.unq.edu.ar/Conflictos_sociales/oconnor_2da_contradiccion.pdf>.

Oxfam. 2016. "Unearthed, land, power and inequality in Latin America." <https://www.oxfam.org/sites/www.oxfam.org/files/file_attachments/bp-land-power-inequality-latin-america-301116-en.pdf>.

Sacher, W. 2016. "Segunda contradicción del capitalismo y megaminería. Reflexiones teóricas y empíricas a partir del caso argentino." Doctoral dissertation. Flacso-Ecuador.

Salama, Pierre. 2011. "China-Brasil: industrialización y 'desindustrialización temprana.'" Open Journal Sistem. <http://www.revistas.unal.edu.co/index.php/ceconomia/article/view/35841/39710>.

Sampere, Joaquim. 2015. "Sobre la revolución Rusa y el comunismo del siglo xx." <https://centenarirevoluciorussa.wordpress.com/2015/05/01/31/>.

Svampa, Maristella. 2013. "Resource Extractivism and Alternatives: Latin American Perspectives on Development." In M. Lang and D. Mokrani (eds.), *Beyond Development: Alternative Visions from Latin America*. Amsterdam, The Netherlands: Transnational Institute and Rosa Luxembourg Foundation.

Svampa, Maristella. 2016. *Debates Latinoamericanos*. Indianismo, Desarrollo, Dependencia y Populismo. Buenos Aires: Edhasa.

Svampa, Maristella, and E. Viale. 2014. *Maldesarrollo. La Argentina del extractivismo y el despojo*. Buenos Aires: Editorial Katz.

Terán Mantovani, Emiliano. 2016. "Las nuevas fronteras de las commodities en Venezuela: extractivismo, crisis histórica y disputas territoriales." *Ciencia Política*, 11, 21: 251–285.

2 Socioenvironmental Conflicts and Valuation Languages

This chapter addresses the forces of resistance generated by the capitalist development process on the extractive frontier, examining the different forms and scales of socioenvironmental conflicts. First, I seek to historicize and account for the recursive dynamics of the struggles in different phases of neoextractivism. In this context I also bring into focus the discourse surrounding the notion of territory in terms of what I have described as the ecoterritorial turn, which has been growing along with these struggles.

Neoextractivism as a Phase of Capitalist Development

One of the consequences of the current extractivist inflection is an explosion of socioenvironmental conflicts, which is manifest in the ancestral struggles for land and territory carried out by Indigenous and peasant movements, as well as in the emergence of new forms of mobilization and citizen participation centred in the defence of the commons, biodiversity and the environment. With reference to its characteristics (social fragmentation, displacement of other forms of economy, verticality of decisions, strong impact on ecosystems) rather than its consequences, conflict can be seen as inherent to neoextractivism, even if in some cases social resistance does not translate into conflict.

In referring to socioenvironmental conflicts, I have in mind those that are linked to diverse struggles to control or limit access to the commons and the demand of communities to have companies and governments respect their territorial rights.[1] These conflicts express different conceptions of territory, nature and the environment. In certain cases, to the extent that multiple megaprojects tend to reconfigure disputed territories, conflicts often end up as a dispute about what is meant by development and, more generally, other forms of democracy — participatory, social and direct. Over the years in the new millennium, as capital has found new ways to expand on the extractive frontier, socioenvironmental conflicts have multiplied while social resistance has become more active and organized. Here I distinguish three phases of neoextractivism.

The first is the phase of positivity that unfolded from 2003 to 2008–10. Certainly, at the beginning of this period and during the commodities boom, the extractivist turn was read in terms of the comparative advantages gained by countries in the region exporting their natural resource wealth in primary commodity form — the "new developmentalism," which went beyond differences between progressive and conservative governments. I highlight the fact that it was a positivity phase because the increase in social spending and its impact on poverty reduction, the growing role of the state and the broadening of popular participation generated great political expectations in the wider society, especially after successive crises and decades of economic stagnation and neoliberal adjustment. It should not be forgotten that between 2002 and 2011 poverty in the region was reduced from 44 to 31.4 percent while extreme poverty fell from 19.4 to 12.3 percent (CEPAL 2013). Most countries in the region adopted the new social policy of poverty reduction and extended a battery of social programs reaching 19 percent of the population (i.e., some 120 million people; CEPAL 2014).

This first phase was also characterized by an expansion of the boundaries of state-sanctioned law, manifest in the constitutionalization of new rights (individual and collective, basic human rights, territorial rights and the rights of nature). As seen in the cases of Bolivia and Ecuador, the statist narrative, with its diverse articulations and inner tensions, has coexisted with an indigenist and ecologist narrative. However, throughout the decade and amid the different territorial and socioenvironmental conflicts and their recursive dynamics, the so-called progressive governments ended up adopting a belligerently developmentalist discourse in defence of neoextractivism, accompanied by a criminalizing and tendentiously repressive practice against community activists, branding them as "environmental terrorists."

This period of economic boom and the reformulation of the role of the state was also a period of low visibility, even of non-recognition, of the conflicts associated with the extractive dynamics that lasted approximately until 2008–10, when the progressive governments, having established their respective mandates (many of them having renewed presidential mandates), articulated an explicitly extractivist matrix in the context of virulent territorial and socioenvironmental conflicts. Moreover, the outbreak of conflict related to extractive activities (mega-mining, mega-oil, expansion of the agrarian frontier) highlighted the alliances that are inherent in hegemonic development, the limitations imposed on citizen participation processes and the criminalization of the struggle waged by community activists against the advance and destructive operations of extractive capital.

The second phase corresponds to the proliferation of megaprojects as well as the expansion of social resistance. As with the former, this is reflected in the national development plans submitted by the different governments that were explicitly pursuing a progressive postneoliberal policy agenda. The emphasis in each and all cases was on an increase of different extractive activities — the extraction of minerals or oil, implementation of hydroelectric power stations or expansion of transgenic crops — according to the specialization of the country. In the case of Brazil, the manifestation of this development ment was the Growth Acceleration Program, which launched in 2007 and envisaged the construction of a large number of dams in the Amazon, in addition to the realization of energy megaprojects linked to the exploitation of oil and the gas. In the case of Bolivia, it was the promise of a great industrial leap forward, based on the proliferation of projects involving the extraction of gas, lithium and iron and the expansion of agribusiness, among others. For Ecuador, it meant the approval of open-pit mega-mining projects and the expansion of the oil frontier. For Venezuela, it entailed a strategic plan for oil production, which involved an advance of the exploitation frontier in the Orinoco belt. As for Argentina, it included the 2010–20 Agri-food Strategic Plan, which projected a 60 percent increase in grain production, as well as a commitment to fracking. Thus, even when the commitment to an extractivist strategy was framed by reference to an allegedly industrialist rhetoric, the public policies of the different governments caught up in the progressive cycle were designed to deepen the neoextractivist model, in the context of the commodities boom and a period of high economic growth and extraordinary profitability.[2]

This increase in megaprojects also manifested through the Initiative for the Integration of Regional Infrastructure in South America (IIRSA), later called the South American Infrastructure and Planning Council (Cosiplan), which covers transport projects (waterways, ports, bi-oceanic corridors and others), energy (large hydroelectric dams) and communications. This program was agreed to in 2000 by several Latin American governments, whose main objective was to facilitate the extraction and export of products to their destination ports. In 2007, IIRSA came under the control of the Union of South American Nations (UNASUR). According to researcher

Silvia Carpio (2017) of the Centro de Estudios para el Desarrollo Laboral y Agrario , the main promoter of UNASUR and Cosiplan was the president of Brazil, Lula da Silva, who sought to strengthen ties with other countries in South America through the intensification of regional trade and investments in infrastructure works by the Brazilian Development Bank. The IIRSA-Cosiplan projects have faced resistance and questioning in various regions because, despite the rhetoric about the need to "weave new relations between states, peoples and communities" through infrastructure integration in Latin America, they are actually guided by market objectives, with 544 projects totalling an estimated investment of 130,000 million dollars.

By 2014, 32.3 percent of investments within IIRSA were in the area of energy, concentrated mainly in hydroelectric power plants, which have been highly questioned in regard to their negative social and environmental impacts, especially in the already fragile zone of the Brazilian and Bolivian Amazon (Carpio 2017). Furthermore, of thirty-one Cosiplan priority projects, fourteen touch the Amazon (Porto 2017: 158).

This second stage brings us into a period of "whitewashing" the Commodities Consensus — that is, of open conflict in extractive territories. Indeed, numerous local socioenvironmental and territorial conflicts acquired national visibility, including those related to the building of a highway through Isiboro Sécure National Park and Indigenous Territory (Tipnis) in Bolivia, the construction of the Belo Monte mega-dam in Brazil, threats of mega-mining and the resulting 2012 insurrection in Famatina, Argentina, and finally the suspension in 2013 of Ecuador's proposal to ban oil drilling in Yasuní National Park. What is clear is that the expansion of rights (collective, territorial, environmental) found a limit in the growing expansion of the exploitation of capital in search of goods, lands and territories, which overturned the emancipatory narratives that had raised high expectations, especially in countries such as Bolivia and Ecuador.

To these emblematic conflicts in countries with progressive governments must be added those that occurred along the same lines under governments of a neoliberal or conservative nature. Such was the case of the Conga mining project in Peru, discontinued as the result of popular resistance and violent conflict between local communities and the government, which had taken the side of the companies involved against the communities. There was a similar outcome in regard to the mining megaproject La Colosa in the department of Tolima in Colombia, which was finally suspended in 2017, and the project of the Agua Zarca dam on the Gualcarque River in Honduras, which was suspended thanks to the action of the Civic Council of Popular and Indigenous Organizations of Honduras (COPINH).

In short, in the midst of the different territorial and environmental conflicts and their recursive dynamics, Latin American governments ended up adopting a belligerently developmentalist discourse in defence of neoextractivism, accompanying their productivist and El Dorado–inspired narratives with an open practice of criminalizing resistance. The openness of this discourse and practice occurred even in those countries that had the highest political expectations of change, including Ecuador and Bolivia, which had made political commitments to bring about a condition of *buen vivir* in social solidarity and harmony with nature — a commitment enshrined in both cases in a new constitution that founded a plurinational, multiethnic state. The actual political practice of both governments — as opposed to the radical postdevelopment rhetoric of *buen vivir* — illustrated the evolution of governments forged in the heat of the progressive cycle towards traditional models and a retraction of the commitment to a more popular form of democracy, manifest in the evident intolerance of dissidence.

Certainly, one of the elements present in the different progressive governments was the stigmatization of environmental protest; in some cases, it took the form of conspiracy theories about foreign interests acting through protesters. In fact, where an environmental and territorial conflict attracted media attention, was politicized and highlighted the blind spots of the progressive governments regarding the dynamics of dispossession, authorities unanimously reacted by rejecting any concerns. By 2009 this had happened in Ecuador, especially with respect to mega-mining; in Brazil, as a result of the conflict caused by the construction of the Belo Monte Dam; and in Bolivia, with respect to the government's plan to construct a road through Tipnis, the national heritage park occupied by diverse Indigenous groups and communities that were vehemently opposed to the project. In all three cases, the different governments opted for nationalist language and avoided the real issue, denying the legitimacy of the concerns raised and attributing them to environmentalist infantilism (Ecuador), the actions of foreign NGOs (Brazil) or colonial environmentalism (Bolivia). The Tipnis conflict was particularly resonant in the annals of popular resistance. Although there were several episodes that anticipated a collision between the indigenist narrative and extractivist practice, the turning point occurred in 2010–11, following the construction of the Villa Tunari-San Ignacio de Moxos highway. Since 1965 the Tipnis has been a natural reserve and since 1990 it has been recognized as an Indigenous territory, the habitat of Amazonian peoples. The issue that brought the government into conflict with Indigenous Peoples here was undoubtedly complex, because, on the one hand, the road responded to geopolitical and territorial needs, and on the other hand, the central issue was that the Indigenous Peoples involved were not consulted. Also, with or without Brazil as a strategic ally on the project, all indications were that the road would open the door to extractive projects, with negative social, cultural and environmental consequences. The escalation of the conflict between Indigenous organizations and environmentalists versus the government was such that it included several marches from the Tipnis to the city of La Paz, in addition to a dark repressive episode and the formation of a multisectoral alliance between rural, social and Indigenous organizations and environmentalists, with the support of huge urban sectors. In 2012 the government of Evo Morales called for a consultation with the Indigenous communities of Tipnis. The official report of this consultation indicated that 80 percent of the communities consulted approved the construction of the highway — which was difficult to reconcile with the record of protest and active mobilizations led by the Indigenous communities in the disputed territory. A report from the Catholic Church, carried out together with the Permanent Assembly for Human Rights of Bolivia in April 2013, indicated that the consultation "was not free or in good faith, and in addition it did not conform to the standards of prior consultation and it was carried out with perks."[3]

The Tipnis conflict realized two important conclusions that must be read in the context of Bolivia but also Latin America. First, as the conflict advanced, the government whitewashed its discourse regarding what it understood by development, something that Bolivian Vice President A. García Linera, in his book *Geopolítica de la Amazonía* (2012), was commissioned to do. For Linera, without extractivism there would be no way to sustain the government's social policies, which would mean the failure of the government and the inevitable restoration of the Right. Second, amid escalating conflict, in a virulent and politicized context where the recursive nature of the action led to different actors getting involved in a fierce struggle, the likelihood of carrying out free, prior and informed consultations with Indigenous Peoples as established by Convention 169 of the International Labour Organization was very low. Also, the question of how to proceed with the government's plan for the Tipnis became highly controversial.

Finally, in continuity with the second phase of the extractivist cycle — from 2013–15 up to the present when the primary commodities boom on the world market collapsed — we are currently witnessing an extension and exacerbation of neoextractivist development strategy. A relevant factor for explaining this phenomenon is precisely the fall in the price of natural resources and raw materials on the world market, which has apparently prompted Latin American governments in the neoextractivist mould to increase the number of extractive projects even more, thus expanding the boundaries of commodity production (Moore 2013; Terán 2016). In this context, the majority of Latin American governments were evidently not prepared for the fall in commodity prices (see the case of Venezuela), but at the same time they readily saw its consequences in regard to both the trade deficit (Martínez Alier 2015) and a recessive economic growth trend (Peters 2016). To this must be added the decline of the progressive and populist hegemony and the end of the progressive cycle, which will have a strong impact on the reconfiguration of the regional political map, an issue discussed later in the book.

Territory and the New Language of Valuation

At present, there seems to be an implicit consensus among Latin American analysts that one of the constituent dimensions of social resistance against extractivism is the defence of territory and territoriality. Certainly, territory and territoriality are disputed concepts, because they appear not only in the narratives of Indigenous organizations and socioenvironmental movements but also in the discourse of corporations, planners, public policy designers — in short, political power at different scales and levels. In effect, the notion of territory has become a social concept, which allows us to visualize the positioning of the different actors in conflict and, even more, to analyze the social and political dynamics of this conflict.

The appropriation of a territory is never only material; it is also symbolic (Santos 2005). As the Brazilian geographer Bernardo Mançano Fernandes affirms, "We live among various types of productive lands, which are reproduced by different social relations that are disputed on a daily basis" (Fernandes 2008). Undoubtedly, Brazilian critical geography in the tradition of critical development studies has contributed greatly to enriching and updating the concept of territory, especially from a perspective that emphasizes the need to "graph the territories from below" (Porto 2001) — that is, to approximate the sense of territory and territorialization that social movements have in their struggles. For Carlos Porto Gonçalves, our present time can be compared to the Renaissance, insofar as we are witnessing a process of geographical (re)configuration, where the different actors and segments of society do not participate in the same way as in those instituting processes. Territoriality is carried out in a complex space in which logics of action and rationalities that carry different valuations are interwoven. In a similar vein, another Brazilian geographer, Rogério Haesbaert (2011), reflects on the concept of multiterritoriality, which he reads as the counterpart of globalization. In fact, far from being at the end of territory, we have in front of us a more complex multiterritoriality with strong rhizomatic connotations — that is, not hierarchized, and illustrated by territorial networks constructed from below and delineated by subaltern groups.

In general terms, both in urban and rural movements, the territory appears as a space of resistance and also, progressively, as a place of resignification and the creation of new social relations. From a social movement perspective, with reference here to both peasant-Indigenous movements and urban social movements, territoriality in its material dimension has often been understood exclusively as a dimension of community self-organization. However, by the year 2000, the dispute over territory acquired other inflections, such as the desire of companies in the extractive sector to access and exploit land occupied by Indigenous and peasant farming communities, and the demand by these communities for respect regarding their basic human and territorial rights. In this context, extractive megaprojects such as large-scale open-pit mining, the exploration and drilling for oil and gas and the harvesting of agri-food and forest products can be thought of as a paradigmatic example of the shift from a class struggle over land and labour to a socioterritorial struggle for access to the global commons (Porto 2001).

Within the prevailing Commodities Consensus framework, we are witnessing today a return to and a revaluation of the notion of territory as the locus of a wealth of natural resources as well as a habitat and source of subsistence and rural livelihoods. From the perspective of the companies and the governments that view these territories as an "economic opportunity" (a source of productive resources that are highly valued by capital, a potential source of windfall profits or additional fiscal revenues for social development), these lands and territories are "socially empty," or "marginal, empty, under-utilized and available" (Sack 1986). That is, in the name of progress (and invoking the ideology of economic opportunity), the communities settled on these lands are effectively rendered invisible or nonexistent in order to facilitate the entry of other agents and models of development, and to justify governments' concession to capital of the right to invest in the large-scale acquisition of land and extraction of the wealth of natural resources found in these territories for the purpose of capitalist development. For example, in Argentinian Patagonia, vast territories occupied by the Mapuche are considered "desert," which brings back dark reminiscences because the metaphor of a desert was used in the late nineteenth century to corral and exterminate Indigenous populations, devaluing what they represented in terms of culture and habitat. At present, the metaphor of the desert is again used by national and provincial government officials to justify the need for large-scale mining and the expansion of the extractive frontier through fracking or agribusiness as the only way of making productive use of marginal land for the purpose of national development.

Something similar happens with the vast Amazon, another marginalized territory deemed to be virtually "socially empty." As affirmed by Porto (2017), this area is considered to be not only an "inexhaustible source" and "reserve" of valuable resources but also a "demographic void." This vision, which ignores the geographical complexity of the region as well as the productive use of the land by Indigenous communities since time immemorial, is complementary to the characterization of territory as idle or unproductive. In the Latin American context, Peruvian president Alan García expressed this vision starkly in a 2007 article, "El hortelano's dog syndrome" ("The gardener's dog syndrome") published in the traditional newspaper *El Comercio*.[4] In this article he argued that the Amazonian Indians who opposed the exploitation of their "idle" territories were like "the dog of the gardener." He also commented in 2007 that the entire Amazon could be considered an idle territory that had to become efficient and productive through the expansion of extractive capital in the form of mining and exploitation of fossil fuels as a source of energy and industrial development.[5]

In short, the assertion that there are regions historically marked by poverty, social vulnerability and low population density, containing large areas of "unproductive" territories, facilitates the production of a discourse supportive of the global dynamics of capital accumulation. Whether this land and these territories are conceived of as socially empty, idle or empty, the result is the same: the devaluation of other forms of production and the devaluation of regional economies, or the exclusion of other languages of valuation of territory linked to the subaltern sectors and incompatible with the dominant model.

Political-Ideological Matrices and an Ecoterritorial Turn in the Popular Struggle

Before talking about social resistance, it is worth clarifying that there are at least four political-ideological matrices or narratives that contest the discourse of the contemporary political scene in Latin America[6]:the peasant-Indigenous, the national populist movement, the traditional class analysis, and, more recently, the autonomist narrative.

The peasant-Indigenous matrix is placed within the framework of the long history and memory of Indigenous Peoples and is based on the idea of ancestral resistance, collective rights and communal power. In terms of recent history, its evolution is linked to different processes: at the international level with decolonization and the progressive recognition of collective rights (incorporation of International Labour Organization Convention 169 into the different national constitutions, the United Nations Declaration on the Rights of Indigenous Peoples), at the regional level with the crisis of the modernizing developmentalist state and the relative failure to fuse a mestizo-peasant identity and at the national level with the process of an expanding ethnic frontier — that is, the increasingly massive presence of Indigenous People in the cities. In short, the transformation of what in the twentieth century was widely understood as a class struggle over land and labour into what is now viewed as a socioterritorial struggle is in ideological terms reflected in a displacement of Marxist class analysis with a culturalist perspective of identity construction.

Second, another ideological matrix in the field of popular organizations in Latin America is national populism. This ideological matrix relates to the fundamental political experiences of 1930 to 1950, and is sustained with the affirmation of the triple axis of "the nation," the redistributive and conciliatory state, charismatic leadership and "the people" — the organized masses. Although in general the populist matrix combines an appeal to a radical nationalist project with the more classic model of controlled participation, the historical evidence illustrates above all the second model, based on the heteronomy of social movements and labour unionism, following the leader's call, from the state apparatus (resubalternization and the nationalization of social movements).

Third, we must highlight the matrix of social class, which presents a conception of power (and therefore of social change) linked to the idea of class antagonism and the construction of socialism. This matrix nurtures a workerist narrative that includes different variants of partisan and internationalist Marxism, which manifest in different ways in Latin America (linked to the Communist Party, Maoism and the various existing Trotskyisms). This workers' conception of society has traditionally gone against an understanding of the diversity and social heterogeneity existing in peripheral societies. It is no coincidence that historically, when referring to the ability to act autonomously — that is, as a class actor — of subaltern social subjects (peasants, Indigenous communities, marginalized groups, informal workers, rural landless workers and the rural poor), analysts have established the idea that Latin American societies are characterized by weak actors with little class autonomy, who may even be manipulated by other social actors. Hence, tension continues to exist between the class matrix and other narratives in the contestation of theoretical space in the popular struggle.

Fourth, there also exists an autonomist narrative, nourished within the anarchist or autonomist tradition. The central elements that make up this matrix include an affirmation of autonomy, horizontality and democracy by consensus. In this particular case, I refer to a narrative that is constructed as an identity story of the subject's production, in which the personal experience of the actors takes precedence over membership in the community (the peasant-Indigenous matrix), the people (the populist matrix) or social class (the Marxist matrix). Historically, this narrative has been nourished by the general failure of the traditional Left, which is why its definition is important in relation to opposition to other leftist traditions, mainly the Marxist Left. It also appears linked to the processes of deinstitutionalization of contemporary societies and the emergence of new dynamics of individualization. The autonomist narrative has given rise to new models of militancy, disseminated both in the countries at the centre of the world system and in the periphery, whose organizational modality is affinity groups and cultural collectives. Its expansion —in a wide field of environmental and cultural activism, alternative media, popular forms of feminism, antipatriarchal struggle, artistic intervention and popular education — is one of the most emblematic characteristics of the new social movements formed in the latest phase of capitalist development.

With this clarification, we can begin to delineate two processes that reach beyond the specific characteristics of the progressive cycle. On the one hand, from an institutional point of view, with the emergence of progressive governments we have witnessed a political dynamic that with different nuances and gradations led to the nationalization of numerous social movements, a space in which the populist matrix emerged as hegemonic. In other words, during the progressive cycle, the new form of the populist matrix was seen in a growing hegemonic dynamic based on the rejection and absorption of elements from other competing matrices — the peasant-Indigenous narrative, the new autonomous Left — that had played an important role at the beginning.

On the other hand, as of 2003 the socioenvironmental struggle laid the foundations of a common language of valuation of territoriality, what I have termed the ecoterritorial turn, which is manifest in the convergence of different matrices and languages and an innovative crossing between the peasant-Indigenous and autonomist narratives, bound by an environmental thread, which by the end of the cycle had also added a feminist thread. As a result, a common narrative emerged that focused on the defence of land and territory and sought to account for the way in which current socioenvironmental struggles are thought of and represented. The ecoterritorial turn refers to the construction of various frames of collective action that also function as structures of meaning and schemes of alternative interpretation.[7] These collective frameworks tend to develop an important mobilizing capacity, and establish new themes, languages and slogans in societal debates while orienting the interactive dynamic towards the production of a common subjectivity in spaces of resistance.

The consolidation of an alternative language of valuation in contrast to the dominant view of territoriality seems to be more immediate in the case of Indigenous and peasant organizations, due to the close relationship they see between land and territory in terms of the interrelation of human life with nature. However, far from being exclusive to those countries with a notable presence of historically excluded Indigenous Peoples and communities, the ecoterritorial shift is also found in other countries, where it manifests through different multiethnic experiences and diverse organizational formats.

Socioenvironmental Conflicts and Their Scales

The explosion of socioenvironmental conflicts had as a correlate what renowned Mexican essayist Enrique Leff has described as "the environmentalization of indigenous and peasant struggles and the emergence of Latin American environmental thought" (Leff 2004). To this we must add that the scenario is marked not only by peasant-Indigenous struggles but also by the emergence of new socioenvironmental movements and multi-class rural and urban movements in small and medium-sized towns. At the same time, in this context (and social fabric), a different role is played by certain cultural collectives, environmental NGOs (within the logic of social movements), intellectuals and experts, who accompany and even participate in the interactions and collaborations between organizations, communities and movements in the popular sector and the extractive frontier. As often happens in other fields of struggle, the organizational dynamic of collective action includes youth and women as central actors. The role of women in both the large organizational structures and the small groups that support collective actions of resistance is crucial.

The crossings and intersections between organizations have given rise to numerous spaces for coordinated collective action (such as Vía Campesina) or, at a different level and scale, thematic forums (such as the defence of water, the defence of natural resources, opposition to fracking) and platforms of joint actions (against the Free Trade Area of the Americas, against the IIRSA megaprojects and more recently against the Trans-Pacific Partnership).

In this sense, the most novel thing is the collaboration between different actors, which promotes a dialogue of knowledge and discipline, character-ized by the valorization of local knowledge as well as the elaboration of an expert knowledge independent of dominant discourses. This is not a minor issue, since this collaboration of different organizations and movements has resulted in the elaboration of common diagnoses, extension of the discursive platform that exceeds the local and national problematic and diversification of strategies of struggle, combining the mobilization of the social base and the collaboration of diverse social networks with the generation and applica-tion of different technical and legal instruments (collective protection, new ordinances, demand for public consultation and laws for the protection of the environment and the rights of Indigenous Peoples).

Of all the extractive activities undertaken and underway in Latin America, the most questioned and heavily criticized is undoubtedly large-scale metal mining. At the moment there is not one Latin American country with mining projects where communities are not brought into a relation of conflict with the mining companies — and often, the government takes the side of capital in these struggles. This is the case, for example, in Mexico, Guatemala, El Salvador, Honduras, Costa Rica, Panama, Ecuador, Peru, Colombia, Brazil, Argentina and Chile. There are several organiza-tional spaces dedicated to the issue of mining — among them are the Latin American Observatory of Environmental Conflicts, which was created in 1991 and has its headquarters in Chile, and the Observatory of Mining Conflicts in Latin America (OCMAL), which has been in operation since 1997 and brings together more than forty organizations, including Acción Ecológica in Ecuador. According to the OCMAL, in 2010 there were 120 mining conflicts that affected 150 communities in Latin America; in 2012, there were 161 conflicts, which involved 173 projects and affected 212 com-munities. In February 2014, the number of conflicts in the mining sector was 198, affecting 297 communities and involving 207 projects. In January 2017, there were 217 conflicts, involving 227 projects and 331 communities. The countries with the greatest number of conflicts in 2017 were Peru (39), Mexico (37), Chile (36), Argentina (26), Brazil (20), Colombia (14) and Ecuador (7). Six conflicts are cross-border. According to the Environmental Justice Atlas, the level and number of conflicts increased in 1997 and again in 2006–08.[8] OCMAL also showed an increase in conflict in this timeframe (Villegas 2014: 10–11).

It is impossible to carry out a survey of socioenvironmental conflicts or a list of the self-organizing national and regional environmental networks that now exist in Latin America. Without claiming any exhaustiveness and only by way of example, I provide a brief review of some conflicts and networks in Peru, Bolivia, Nicaragua, Ecuador, Colombia, Mexico and Argentina.[9] In 2013 in Peru, a country with a tradition of large-scale mining, out of a total of 120 conflicts, 48 percent were linked to mining, according to the Ombudsman's Office (Álvarez and Bottaro 2013; Machado 2013, 2014).[10] In 2016, the percentage had risen to 68, since there were 220 social conflicts identified by the Peruvian authorities throughout the national territory, and 150 of these were related to mining projects (Contralínea 2016). Among the pioneering organizations at the continental level in the fight against mega-mining, the National Confederation of Peruvian Communities Affected by Mining (Conacami), born in 1999, stands out. At present, although Conacami no longer has the territorial presence and coordianting capacity that it once had, in its place other local organizational structures, such as the peasant patrols (rondas campesinas), whose role is to lead the fight against mega-mining, have emerged and been strengthened (Hoetmer et al. 2013: 268). Another important organization is the Training and Intervention Group for Sustainable Development of Cajamarca, Peru, which has a long history of intervention and struggle, and whose leader, former priest and sociologist Marco Arana, founded the Tierra y Libertad party in 2009.[11]

In Bolivia, the extractivist wave includes mining, hydrocarbon exploitation, agribusiness and, more recently, a series of energy projects included in the so-called 2025 Patriotic Agenda and the new national development plan, which involves the construction of several mega-dams and a nuclear power plant in El Alto. As noted, the watershed was the Tipnis conflict over the construction of a road through a nature reserve and Indigenous territory. Vice President Álvaro García Linera assumed the responsibility and task of defending extractivism, and in 2015 he threatened to expel from the country four Bolivian NGOs (Documentation and Information Centre of Bolivia, Fundación Terra, Centro de Estudios para el Desarrollo Laboral y Agrario, and Milenio), several of which carry out research on neoextractivism and the expansion of the agribusiness frontier, accusing them of defending "the interests of the international political right."[12] In 2016, the government enacted a new law, which aims to restrict freedom of association and puts critical NGOs at risk of closure if they do not comply with the 2025 Patriotic Agenda and the national development plan. In 2017, the increasing harassment and persecution of the Documentation and Information Centre of Bolivia made its operations almost untenable.

One of the most worrisome cases is Ecuador, where, despite the fact that the constitution establishes the rights of nature, the response of the Correa government to socioenvironmental conflicts between communities and companies was to criminalize and prosecute protest actions through criminal trials of spokespeople of Indigenous organizations, with a jail sentence of ten years.[13] The government response also included the withdrawal of legal status and the expulsion from the country of some NGOs such as the Fundación Pachamama (2013), harassment and a threat to dissolve the recognized NGO Acción Ecológica (in both 2009 and 2016) and visa cancellation and expulsion of foreign consultants linked to environmental activism (2014 and 2015).

The Ecuadorian government also used legal devices to invalidate the Yasuní-ITT Initiative, which had been proposed by the Yasunidos citizen movement, unilaterally deciding to end the moratorium on drilling in Yasuní Park. Despite the significant resistance to mega-mining (Ecuador has no tradition of large-scale mining), from 2013 onwards the government has increased the military presence in the mining regions, including Intag, a stronghold in the fight against this type of activity, where the population had expelled several mining companies and opted for alternative forms of development.

Further, the Chinese companies that now lead mining investment in the country have been accused of abusive labour practices.[14] According to Acción Ecológica, in 2012 Chinese companies linked to the Mirador mining project were denounced by the Indigenous Shuar community for failure to provide promised employment benefits, mistreatment, unfair wages and accidents. In 2016, there was new conflict when Shuar people took over a mining camp in the Amazon region that had been established by a Chinese company without prior consultation and by militarizing the area. In December of that year, faced with opposition from the Shuar community, the conflict escalated to the point that there was one death and several wounded. The response of President Correa was to declare a state of emergency, accusing the Shuar of forming "paramilitary and semi-criminal groups" and announcing the dissolution of Acción Ecológica. Finally, as a result of national and international solidarity, Ecuador's Ministry of Environment rejected the request for dissolution sent by the Ministry of the Interior.

Likewise, in Colombia from 2001 to 2011, 25 percent of conflicts were related to the extraction of oil, gold or coal (Roa and Navas 2014: 35). In 2010, during his first presidential campaign, Manuel Santos presented the slogan "Colombia, the mining and energy locomotive." One mining project that aroused enormous resistance is La Colosa, run by the company Anglo Gold Ashanti, which, if it had been built, would have become the fifth-largest gold mine in the world, affecting many localities in the department of

Tolima, considered the agricultural pantry of Colombia. There, local activists created environmental committees in defence of life, which prompted public consultations. After a first consultation in the town of Piedras in 2013, the environmental committees set out to organize consultations in Cajamarca and Ibague but encountered serious legal and business obstacles. Finally, in April 2017 a public consultation was held in Cajamarca, which also produced a negative result for La Colosa. That same year, in the absence of a social licence, Anglo Gold Ashanti decided to suspend all project activities.[15]

But mega-mining is not the only front of neoextractivist conflict in Colombia. There is also the Master Plan for the Exploitation of the Magdalena River, the most important river in the country, which originates in the Andes and travels for 1,500 kilometres. This is part of IIRSA policy, which, far from improving the environmental and social conditions of the river, aims to convert it into a large waterway to transport coal, oil and palm leaf for export via deep draft vessels. The other objective is to turn it into a great generator of energy through the construction of several dams, many of which would be at the service of mining projects. This enormous plan to privatize the river (made with a company of Chinese origin) provoked a mobilization that took the name of the River of Life.

In Mexico, the National Assembly of the Environmentally Affected was created in 2008 to resist mega-mining, hydroelectric dams, so-called "wild urbanization" and industrial mega-farms. For ten years, the Council of Ejidos and Opposition Communities to the La Parota Dam brought together the struggles of Indigenous peasants in Guerrero under the slogan "We are the custodians of water" (Navarro 2015: 141). Another important experience is the resistance against the mining company San Xavier by the coalition Frente Amplio Opositor, which led to the mine territory becoming a space for numerous public activities, information rounds, consultations and legal disputes, which culminated in 2006 when the company established the mine site where originally it had planned to demolish the town to make way for operations (Composto and Navarro 2011: 51).

Nicaragua has one of the most ambitious and controversial megaprojects in the region. The concession for the Interoceanic Canal, which would be three times larger than the Panama Canal, was granted to the Chinese company HKND. The first protest by affected communities occurred in 2014. In November 2015, initial work on the canal was postponed due to peasant protests and questioning of the environmental impact study by international experts convened by the Academy of Sciences of Nicaragua. As a consequence, the National Council for the Defence of Land, Lake and Sovereignty was born. At the end of 2016, a peasant march against the project that was intended to reach Managua was repressed by the police and the military, resulting in numerous bullet wounds and detainees. For the time being, work has not been able to start on the canal, which would affect numerous communities and have serious impacts on Lake Nicaragua, the largest freshwater reserve in the region.

Finally, in Argentina, popular assemblies that were formed in a number of urban municipalities in defence of water and unified in the form of the Union of Citizen Assemblies were originally linked to the fight against mega-mining, and to a lesser extent a critique of the corporate agribusiness model. The Union of Citizen Assemblies, established in 2006, has an assembly format and meets three times a year, with the aim of designing common strategies of resistance against the advance of the mining model in twelve provinces and defending the provincial laws (seven in total) that prohibit mega-mining in that country. In respect to agribusiness, which is linked to the expansion of transgenic soybeans, the heart of agrarian capitalism in Argentina, resistance was more difficult to manifest, despite the pioneering role of the Madres del Barrio Ituzaingó in the province of Córdoba. Since 2007 there has been a "Stop Fumigating" campaign promoted by the Nature Protection Centre of Santa Fe, the Rural Reflection Group and other groups (Melón 2014: 79). In bringing public attention to the issues, the role of physicians and researchers, such as Andrés Carrasco and other professionals who created the Red de Médicos de Pueblos Fumigados (Network of Doctors from Fumigated Villages), has been crucial.[16]

NOTES

1. Recalling Fontaine's (2003) definition, to which I add the asymmetric character of the struggles.
2. Editor's note. The caveat here is that this profitability was experienced primarily by foreign investors and the companies that were given concessions and thirty-plus-year contracts to explore for and extract this natural resource wealth for the purpose of exporting it in primary commodity form. Several studies on the global exploitation chain of extractive capital have shown that while capital experienced profit rates of up to 60 percent on invested capital, in most cases less than 20 percent of the value of the natural resources on the world market accrued to workers and the governments in the form of resource rents (export taxes, royalties; Veltmeyer and Petras 2014).
3. <https://cedib.org/post_type_titulares/obispos-defienden-su-informe-de-la-consulta-previa-en-el-tipnis-pagina-7-15-04-13>.
4. <http://peruesmas.com/biblioteca-jorge/Alan-Garcia-Perez-y-el-perro-del-hortelano.pdf>.
5. This comment, made in 2007, became widely known in June 2008, when Peru's

executive sanctioned a hundred legislative decrees, including a package of eleven laws affecting the Amazon. Legislative decrees, which were renamed "the law of the jungle" by Indigenous organizations and environmental NGOs, were questioned by different sectors. On June 5, 2009, state repression in the area of Bagua cost the lives of some thirty inhabitants of the Amazon region and ten police officers, and resulted in an unknown number of disappeared persons.

6. By "political-ideological matrices" I mean those guidelines that organize the way of thinking about politics and power, as well as conceptions of social change. Although each political-ideological matrix has a specific configuration, the different national contexts as well as the internal tensions endow them, in each case, with a dynamism and a particular historicity. On the other hand, the political-ideological matrices to which I refer are not discrete, because the different political dynamics have given way to various intersections and conjunctions (between Indianism and Marxism, between indigenism and a populist matrix, between indigenism and autonomist narrative, between Marxism and autonomism, to give some examples), as well as a process of conflict and collision, which can lead to accentuating differences in terms of ways of doing politics and conceptions of social change. See Svampa (2010, 2017).

7. Erving Goffman defined frames as "interpretation schemes that enable individuals and groups to locate, perceive, identify and name the facts of their own world and the world in general" (Goffman 1974). For Gamson, the frames are defined by three basic elements: the frame of (in)justice, the capacity of agency and work on the identity (they/us). From a constructivist and interactionist perspective, however, there are different approaches to "framing processes" (see Meyer and Gamson 1992). In this vein, I should clarify that I do not subscribe to a purely instrumental approach in the use of collective frameworks but rather a cultural and moral approach linked to the framework of injustice.

8. The Environmental Justice Atlas <https://ejatlas.org> is a project in which an international team of experts from twenty-three universities and environmental justice organizations from eighteen countries participate. It is coordinated by researchers from the Institute of Science and Technology at the Autonomous University of Barcelona, under the direction of Joan Martínez Alier. At the same time, it is a collective project in which civil society is a participant.

9. There is a huge bibliography on socioenvironmental conflicts at the national level that are linked to extractivism in Latin America. In the case of Peru, I recommend the texts of De Echave et al. (2009) and Hoetmer et al. (2013), which articulate counterexpert knowledge with a view from social movements against mega-mining. For the case of Bolivia, see the work of the Documentation and Information Centre of Bolivia from 2014 onward <https://www.cedib.org/biblioteca/materiales-digitales/documentos/>; for Colombia, see Roa and Navas (2014) and Archila (2015); for Mexico, see Composto and Navarro (2011) and Navarro (2015), as well as Delgado (2010) and Lemus (2018). For a mapping of environmental conflicts in Argentina, see Merlinsky (2016), Giarracca and Teubal (2013) and Svampa and Viale (2014).

10. <http://www.defensoria.gob.pe/blog/mineria-y-conflictos/>.

11. This party, renamed Tierra y Dignidad (Land and Dignity), participated in the Frente Amplio coalition, which came third in the 2016 general election with the candidacy of Verónika Mendoza.

12. See the public letter of intellectuals to Vice President García Linera at <https://www.eldeber.com.bo/bolivia/31-intelectuales-del-mundo-piden-a-Garcia-Linera-respeto-a-las-ONG-20150813-46651.html>.

13. See the report of the International Federation of Human Rights (2015), which includes cases of criminalization of defenders of human rights in Latin America. Among these are the cases of criminalization in Intag and of the Indigenous people of the Shuar Federation. On this see <https://www.fidh.org/img/pdf/criminalisation-20 sangocto2015bassdef.pdf>.

14. Chinese companies provide numerous benefits, since "they execute the projects financed with Chinese credits granted with high interest rates and, in addition, normally the payment is subject to inputs that they themselves provide and to the hiring of Chinese labour." Consult <http://catapa.be/es/noticias/ el-cuento-de-la-miner%C3%ada-china-en-ecuador>. For the issue of mining and the presence of Chinese companies in Ecuador, see Chicaiza (2014) and Sacher (2016).

15. In recent years, in a context of loosened environmental controls, Anglo Gold Ashanti, a company of South African origin but with a majority of US and British shareholders, came to possess — through uncertain methods — titles to mine rights across the region, many of those in areas where people were being displaced by guerrillas and paramilitaries. This went almost unnoticed in Colombian society.

16. In 2009, Dr. Andrés Carrasco, professor of embryology, principal investigator of the National Council of Scientific and Technical Research (Conicet) and director of the Molecular Embryology Laboratory of the Faculty of Medicine of the University of Buenos Aires and Conicet, presented his research on the harmful effects of the agrochemical glyphosate on embryos, proving that, with doses up to 1,500 times lower than those used in the fumigations that are carried out on Argentinian fields, there were intestinal and cardiac disorders, malformations and neuronal alterations. A defamation campaign against Carrasco had several repercussions (anonymous threats, media and institutional discrediting campaigns, strong political pressures), which generated a declaration of support signed by more than three hundred researchers and colleagues at the national and international levels in defence of the freedom of investigation and public ethics. The situation of harassment and intolerance has been aggravated by the increasingly clear results of independent scientific research in the field of agrochemicals and genetically modified organisms.

REFERENCES

Archila, Mauricio (coord.). 2015. "'Hasta cuando soñemos': Extractivismo e interculturalidad en el sur de la Guajira." Bogota: CINEP/Programa por la Paz.

Álvarez, Sola, and Lorena Bottaro. 2013. "La expansión del extractivismo y los conflictos socioambientales en torno a la megaminería a cielo abierto en Argentina." *Revista latinoamericana PACARINA de Ciencias Sociales y Humanidades,*

4: 89–100.

Carpio, Silvia. 2017. "Integración energética sudamericana: entre la realidad, perspectivas e incertidumbres." In *Discursos y realidades*. *Matriz energética, políticas e integración*. *Plataforma Energética*, 91–138. Bolivia: Centro de Estudios para el Desarrollo Laboral y Agrario.

CEPAL. 2013. *Anuario Estadístico de América Latina y el Caribe*. Santiago de Chile: CEPAL.

CEPAL. 2014. *Anuario Estadístico de América Latina y el Caribe*. Santiago de Chile: CEPAL.

Chicaiza, Gloria. 2014. *Mineras chinas en Ecuador: Nueva dependencia*. Quito: Agencia Ecologista de la Información.

Composto, Claudia, and Mina Lorena Navarro. 2011. "Territorios en disputa: entre el despojo y las resistencias. La megaminería en México." Entender la descomposición, vislumbrar las posibilidades, México.

Contralínea. 2016. "Perú: 150 conflictos mineros." <http://www.contralinea.com. mx/archivo-revista/index.php/2016/09/16/peru-150-conflictos-mineros/>.

De Echave, José, Alejandro Diez, Ludwig Huber, Bruno Revesz, Xavier Ricard Lanata and Martín TanaKa. 2009. *Minería y Conflicto social*. Lima: IEP-Cipca.

Delgado, Gian Carlo. 2010. *Ecología Política de la minería en América Latina: Aspectos socioeconómicos, legales y ambientales de la mega minería*. México: Centro de Investigaciones Interdisciplinarias en Ciencias y Humanidades, UNAM.

Fernandes, Bernardo Mançano. 2008. "Sobre la tipología de los territorios." <https:// web.ua.es/es/giecryal/documentos/documentos839/docs/bernardo-tipologia-de-territorios-espanol.pdf>.

Fontaine, Guillaume. 2003. "Enfoques conceptuales y metodológicos para una sociología de los conflictos ambientales, escrito a propósito del petróleo y los grupos étnicos en la región amazónica." <http://library.fes.de/pdf-files/bueros/ kolumbien/01993/12.pdf>.

Giarracca, Norma, and Miguel Teubal (eds.). 2013. *Actividades extractivas en expansión. ¿Reprimarización de la economía argentina?* Buenos Aires: Antropofagia.

Goffman, Erving. 1974. *Frame Analysis: An Essay on the Organization of Experience*. Harvard University Press.

Haesbaert, Rogério. 2011. *El mito de la desterritorialización. Del "fin de los territorios a la multiterritorialidad."* México: Siglo xxi.

Hoetmer, Raphael, Miguel Castro, Mar Daza and José de Echave. 2013. *Minería y Movimientos sociales en el Perú. Instrumentos y propuestas para la defensa de la vida, el agua y los territorios*. La: Cooper-acción, PDGT.

Leff, Enrique. 2004. "La ecología política en América Latina: un campo de construcción." In Héctor Alimonda (ed.), *Los tormentos de la materia. Aportes para una ecología política latinoamericana*. Buenos Aires: Ediciones de Clacso.

Lemus, Jesús J. 2018. *México a cielo abierto. De cómo el boom minero resquebrajó al país*. México: Grijalbo.

Linera, Alvaro García. 2012. *Geopolítica de la Amazonia*. Bolivia: Vicepresidencia del Estado Plurinacional.

Machado Aráoz, Horacio. 2013. "Crisis ecológica, conflictos socioambientales y orden neocolonial. Las paradojas de Nuestra América en las fronteras del extractivismo." *Revista Brasileira de Estudos Latino-Americanos*, 3, 1: 118–155. <http://rebela.edugraf.ufsc.br/index.php/pc/article/ view/137>.

Machado Aráoz, Horacio. 2014. *Potosí, el origen*. Buenos Aires: Mardulce.

Martínez Alier, J. 2015. "El triunfo del posextractivismo en 2015." Sinpermiso. <http://www.sinpermiso.info/textos/index.php?id=7778>.

Melón, Daiana (coord.). 2014. *La patria sojera: El modelo agrosojero en el Cono Sur*. Buenos Aires: Editorial El Colectivo.

Merlinsky, Gabriela (ed.). 2016. *Cartografías del conflicto ambiental en Argentina*. Buenos Aires: Ciccus-Clacso.

Meyer, David, and William Gamson. 1999. "Marcos interpretativos de la oportunidad política." In Doug McAdam, John McArthy, and Mayer Zald (eds.), *Movimientos Sociales, perspectivas comparadas: oportunidades políticas, estructuras de movilización y marcos interpretativos culturales*. Madrid: Ediciones Istmo.

Modonesi, M. 2016. "Subalternización y revolución pasiva." In *El principio antagonista. Marxismo y acción política*. México: Itaca-UNAM.

Moore, J.W. 2013. "El auge de la ecología-mundo capitalista (ii): las fronteras mercantiles en el auge y decadencia de la apropiación máxima." *Filosofía, política y economía en el Laberinto*, 39: 21–30.

Navarro, Mina l. 2015. *Luchas por lo común. Antagonismo social contra el despojo capitalista de los bienes naturales en México*. México: Ediciones Bajo Tierra.

Peters, Stefan. 2016. "Fin del ciclo: el neo-extractivismo en Suramérica frente a la caída de los precios de las materias primas. Un análisis desde una perspectiva de la teoría rentista." In Has-Jurgen Burchardt, Rafael Domínguez, Carlos Larrea and Stefan Peters (eds.), *Nada dura para siempre. Neoextractivismo despús del boom de las materias primas*. Ecuador: Abya Yala.

Porto, C. 2001. *Geografías, Movimientos Sociales. Nuevas Territorialidades y Sustentabilidad*. México: Siglo xxi.

Porto, C. 2017. "Amazonia, Amazonias. Tensiones territoriales actuales." *Nueva Sociedad*, 272: 150–159.

Roa, Tatiana, and Luisa María Navas (eds.). 2014. *Extractivismo, conflictos y resistencias*. Colombia: Censat-Agua Viva-Amigos de la Tierra de Colombia.

Sacher, W. 2016. "Segunda contradicción del capitalismo y megaminería. Reflexiones teóricas y empíricas a partir del caso argentino." Doctoral dissertation. Flacso-Ecuador.

Sack, Robert. 1986. *Human Territoriality: Its Theory and History*. Cambridge: Cambridge University Press.

Santos, M. 2005. "O retorno do territorio." *Reforma agraria y lucha por la tierra en América Latina, territorios y movimientos sociales* vi, 16.

Svampa, Maristella. 2010. *Movimientos Sociales, matrices socio-políticos y nuevos escenarios en América Latina*. Alemania: UniversitaÀàtsbibliothek Kassel.

Svampa, Maristella. 2017. *Del cambio de época al fin de ciclo. Gobiernos Progresistas, extractivismo y movimientos sociales*. Buenos Aires: Edhasa.

Svampa, Maristella, and E. Viale. 2014. *Maldesarrollo. La Argentina del extractivismo y el despojo*. Buenos Aires: Editorial Katz.

Svampa, Maristella, and E. Viale. 2017. "La trumpización de la política ambiental." *Clarín*. <https://www.clarin.com/opinion/trumpizacion-politica-ambiental_0_

Hkctc9bae.html>.

Terán, Emiliano. 2016. "Las nuevas fronteras de las commodities en Venezuela: extractivismo, crisis histórica y disputas territoriales." *Ciencia Política*, 11, 21: 251–285.

Veltmeyer, H., and J. Petras (eds.). 2014. *The New Extractivism: A Post-Neoliberal Development Model or Imperialism of the Twenty-First Century?* London: Zed Books.

Villegas, Pablo N. 2014. "Notas sobre movimientos sociales y gobiernos progresistas." In *Extractivismo: nuevos contextos de dominación y resistencias*, 9–66. Cochabamba: CEDIB.

③ Dimensions of the Ecoterritorial Turn

n this chapter I focus on topics related to the ecoterritorial turn. I point out, first of all, that I understand the ecoterritorial turn as a trend, which means that it is necessary to analyze struggles case by case to see what forms they assume. I also emphasize the dilemmas involved in the recognition of and respect of Indigenous rights, as well as the growing importance of female protagonism. As a result, I highlight the emergence of new popular forms of feminism in the region.

Scope of the Ecoterritorial Turn

The dynamics of socioenvironmental struggles in Latin America have created a common language of valuation regarding territoriality, which increasingly points to the innovative crossing of Indigenous community thinking and the environmentalist discourse. In other words, this convergence is expressed in what I call the ecoterritorial turn, which considers from the perspective of collective resistance how to think about and represent current socioenvironmental struggles. However, when talking about the ecoterritorial turn, I refer to the construction of collective action frames, which work like alternative structures and schemes of interpretation. Such nonconformist frames tend to produce new topics, languages and slogans. Likewise, these frames or schemes of interpretation contribute to the creation of a common collective subjectivity in the Latin American space of struggle.

Having said that, I do not pretend to have encapsulated this idea into an academic concept, but I want to focus on the way in which social movements and organizations give meaning to their struggles. The ecoterritorial turn has significant connections with what the actors themselves call the environmental justice movement, which originated in the 1980s in Black communities in the United States. Actors in other countries who are grouped around this movement understand that the notion of environmental justice involves "the right to a safe, healthy and productive environment for all, where the environment is considered in its entirety, including its ecological, physical, social, political, aesthetic and economic dimensions" (Acselard 2004: 16). This approach emphasizes the unequal distribution of environmental costs, the lack of participation and democracy, and environmental racism towards original peoples; in short, gender injustice and ecological debt are at the heart of diverse environmental justice networks that today are developing across Latin America, in countries such as Chile (Latin American Observatory of Environmental Conflicts) and Brazil (Network of Environmental Justice).[1]

A central concept of the ecoterritorial turn is *buen vivir* (or *vivir bien* in Spanish; in Kichwa, *sumak kawsay*; in Aymara, *sum qamaña*; in Guaraní, *ñandareko*). This utopian concept is a response to a plurality of Indigenous cosmovisions. It would be wrong to claim to encapsulate it in a single vernacular formula attributable to a particular people or culture, or in a new binary scheme that ends up merging with the already established dichotomies of colonial discourse (Lang and Mokrani 2013). This concept postulates new forms of relationship between humans and nature and other human beings (social solidarity). This new civilizational paradigm highlights the need to abandon the idea of development as unlimited economic growth and to opt instead for a solidarity economy and a more sustainable and equitable form of development, as well as a deepening of democracy.

The concept of *buen vivir* has as one of its central axes the integral relationship between humankind and nature. In this way, it involves other valuation languages (ecological, religious, aesthetic, cultural) with respect to nature, and states that economic growth must be subordinated to the preservation of life and recognition of the rights of nature. This vision of an alternative postdevelopment future does not imply an untouched, unspoiled nature but rather a deep respect for the existence of nature and the maintenance and regeneration of its life cycles, structure and evolutionary functions and processes, and a defence of the natural systems that sustain life on this planet (Gudynas 2009). This recognition and profound respect for the rights of nature, which questions the dominant anthropocentric logics (including the logic of capital accumulation) is a vanguard response to the current multifaceted civilizational crisis. In line with the proposal of *buen vivir*, the issue is to construct a society based on a relationship of harmony between humans and nature. So, while development aims to "Westernize" life on the planet, the concept of *buen vivir* redeems the value of diversity and respect for the "other" (Acosta 2011).

Finally, it should be remembered that the debate over the rights of nature was placed on the political agenda by the 2008 Constitution of Ecuador, which established a multi-ethnic and plurinational state and enshrined basic human and territorial rights for Indigenous communities as well as the rights of nature. In the constitution "nature" appears as a subject of rights: "the right to have its existence fully respected, as well as the maintenance and regeneration of its life cycles, structure, functions and evolutionary processes" (Article 71). It must be pointed out that this view of nature, which originated in Latin America, is not held by the majority and has not been shared worldwide.

Another aspect of the ecoterritorial turn is to conceive of the wealth of natural resources as part of the global commons, a key in the search for an alternative paradigm in both the Global North and South. In Latin America, the grammar of the commons can be understood in two senses. On the one hand, in the framework of the fight against different forms of neoextractivism and the extension of the commodification process, the concept of the commons brings into focus the struggle to defend natural resources from the overexploitation and appropriation that occurs via large-scale foreign investments in the acquisition of land — land-grabbing, in the discourse of critical agrarian and development studies — as well as the privatization and commodification of land, water, seeds and other fundamental pillars of rural livelihoods and sources of life. On the other hand, the notion of the commons, or natural resources, also poses a different view on social relationships based on the importance acquired by the spaces and forms of social cooperation, as well as resources of common use and enjoyment. Years ago, Mexican author, post-development advocate and founder of the Universidad de la Tierra (Earth University) Gustavo Esteva (2007) called this space "areas of community."

We must remember that historically peripheral territories have been factories in the production of social solidarity. Located on the margins of the capitalist system, outside the market and in the absence of the state, the popular sector of Latin American society in large part has had to develop and reproduce itself through structures of cooperation and cooperativism, local development and experiments in worker self-management. In the Andean world, the persistence of "community" based on an Indigenous culture of social solidarity as a modality of social relations is a fundamental key to explaining the persistence and recent resurgence of networks of cooperation and interdependence engaged in diverse efforts to construct a social and solidarity economy — mostly in the countryside, where conditions for the reproduction of a communalist culture are more favourable, but also in urban contexts. In the current context of capitalist development, with new enclosures of the commons and the commodification of life, resistance to resource-seeking extractive capital is increasingly taking the form of new community spaces and forms of sociability — that is, a field of experimentation and collective action aimed at reclaiming a community's territorial rights and right of access to the commons, which has evolved as a space of resistance beyond the state and the market.

The different dimensions of the ecoterritorial turn account for the emergence of a new grammar of popular struggle, and the gestation of an alternative language of resistance that provides a common framework for Indigenous struggles and new territorial-ecological and feminist militancies. Whether presented in the language of the defence of territory and the commons, human rights, the rights of nature or *buen vivir*, the demands articulated by the forces of resistance to the advance of extractive capital, and the alternative narratives that embody these demands, point to a democratization of decision-making, even more so in regard to the right of people to say no to projects that seriously affect the living conditions of the more vulnerable sectors and that compromise the prospects of future generations.

However, despite the global impact that this narrative of resistance has had in the struggle against neoliberal globalization, we need to take into account the fact that the new frameworks of discussion have not yet reached the level of societal debate, even if they have managed, with much difficulty, to put different issues on the political agenda. Along these lines, given the heterogeneity of organizations and the tradition of struggle, it would be a mistake to interpret these collective frameworks as if they were univocal or spoke to the collectivity of experiences. In reality, it is necessary to read the ecoterritorial turn as a trend that spans the diverse forces of resistance and informs them from a more general framework. Emblematic socioenvironmental conflicts in the extractive sector (above all in regard to the second phase of neoextractivism) gave the resistance greater visibility and expanded the debate to include environmental problems, even as most governments and not a few urban social sectors did not fully understand the multiple implications of neoextractivism. In short, what we have here are various languages of valuation, which have found social resonance and opened a crack in the Commodities Consensus.

Neoextractivism and Indigenous Peoples

A period of change beginning in 2000, marked by the denaturalization of the relationship between globalization and neoliberalism, created a transitional and conflictive scenario in which one of the major features was the Commodities Consensus, expressed through the (re)union between neoextractivism and a new version of developmentalism. In this way, the crisis of neoliberalism and the relegitimization of critical discourse, as well as the emergence and activism of different social movements, were inserted into a new phase of capitalist development characterized by the advance of resource-seeking extractive capital.

This process of capitalist development, and the expansion of the extractive frontier into Indigenous territories, would have important consequences vis-à-vis the situation of Indigenous Peoples and the increase in socioterritorial conflict. Within the framework of progressive governments, this problematic, read first as tension and later as antagonism, placed Indigenous Peoples at the centre of the conflict in terms of the issue of autonomy and, more generally, the question of their right to prior, free and informed consultation and consent in regard to the operations of extractive capital — and the obligation of extractive companies (mining, energy, agribusiness) to acquire not only government concessions to operate in Indigenous territories but also social licence from the communities on the extractive frontier.

A report by the Economic Commission for Latin America and the Caribbean on the situation of Indigenous Peoples in the period 2009–13, based on the reports of the UN Special Rapporteur on the rights of Indigenous Peoples, stands out as a major nodal point of the diverse conflicts generated by the expansion of extractive activities in Indigenous territories. In the context of these conflicts, the report laments "the breach of the State's responsibility to consult with the indigenous peoples and adopt measures that would protect the indigenous communities before granting concessions to mine for metals or minerals, or drill for oil and gas, and authorizing the execution of extractive projects."[2] This responsibility and these measures were established in the form of Indigenous communities' right to free, prior and informed consent (FPIC). The report also reproduced a mapping of extractive industries that showed that all countries with Indigenous territories experienced socioenvironmental conflicts in these territories. For the period 2010–13, the map identified at least 226 socioenvironmental conflicts associated with mining and fossil fuels projects in the Indigenous territories of Latin America (CEPAL 2014: 139).

However, the implementation of FPIC is complicated by questions of interpretation. Does it involve an obligation just to consult with Indigenous communities or to gain their informed consent as well? And should the results of the consultation be non-binding, or do Indigenous communities have the right to veto projects? The International Labour Organization has determined that consultations must be done in good faith and that their purpose should be to get the consent of the community or at least to reach an agreement. The United Nations Declaration on the Rights of Indigenous Peoples, adopted by the UN General Assembly in 2007, went a step further by invoking the principle of FPIC when it comes to the removal of Indigenous groups from their lands, as well as the approval and application of legislative and administrative measures that affect them. Additionally, the declaration calls for compensation to Indigenous communities for those resources of an intellectual, cultural or spiritual nature that are lost as a result of projects implemented without FPIC. Although these provisions are not binding, they establish a major commitment on the part of states and exert pressure on them to uphold both the human and territorial rights of Indigenous communities.

Along this line, Colombian sociologist and jurist César Rodríguez Garavito distinguishes between strong and weak interpretations of the right of consultation. From his perspective, "international organizations such as the UN Special Rapporteur on the Rights of Indigenous Peoples and the Inter-American Court of Human Rights (2007) have clear interpretations of the demands of international law, especially when these relate to large development or investment plans that have a profound impact on an indigenous people." At the other extreme is the weak procedural conception, such as that expressed by Ecuador's Constitutional Court (Rodríguez Garavito 2012: 48).

At the regional level, there are also other legal tools available, such as the Inter-American Commission on Human Rights (IACHR) of the Organization of American States, which makes binding decisions for member states. Also very important are the reports of the UN Special Rapporteur on human rights and fundamental freedoms of Indigenous Peoples, since they usually give visibility and political force to the demands of Indigenous Peoples through missions to regions in conflict, investigation of ways to overcome obstacles to protecting the rights of Indigenous Peoples and collection of information about violations of these rights. The IACHR has a tradition of strong and effective actions in this regard. So, for example, through an analysis of five cases in dispute, the IACHR in 2007 established an international legal framework to resolve outstanding problems between states and Indigenous communities.

First, the IACHR established that the state is responsible for ensuring the effective participation of Indigenous Peoples. The state has a duty to consult these communities according to customs and traditions, accept and provide information and promote communication between both parties. In addition, consultations must be carried out in good faith through culturally appropriate procedures in the early stages of development projects to make sure that communities are aware of the possible risks. Second, the IACHR provided recommendations on matters on which Indigenous communities should be consulted, among which are the extraction of natural resources in their territories. In addition, it is the communities, not the state, that determine who will represent the Indigenous people in each consultation procedure. Finally, if the development plan is large-scale or has a high impact, the state cannot move forward without obtaining FPIC.

An important advance in this line of interpretation was the judgment of the IACHR on July 30, 2012, in relation to the Kichwa Sarayaku people of the Ecuadorian Amazon. Over a decade ago, a complaint was filed against the Ecuadorian state for having granted an oil concession that allowed an Argentinian-owned company to conduct seismic exploration in the area of the town of Sarayaku without prior consultation. The court determined that Ecuador had violated the rights to prior and informed consultation in regard to Indigenous communal property and to cultural identity. The state was also held responsible for seriously endangering the rights to life and personal integrity and for violating the guarantees and protections afforded by the country's constitution, to the detriment of the Sarayaku people. As a result, the court ordered Ecuador "to withdraw the pentolite from the territory of the Sarayaku People."[3] In addition, the court ordered the state to conduct an adequate, effective and full consultation before starting any natural resource extraction project. The government must also provide mandatory courses on the rights of Indigenous Peoples for officials whose work involves Indigenous Peoples, as well as organize "a public act of recognition of their responsibility for the violations." Finally, the court established that the state had to pay US$90,000 in material damages and US$1,250,000 for non-material damages to the town of Sarayaku.[4]

This ruling marked a milestone on the matter and was expected to have an impact on pending litigation regarding Indigenous rights and the expansion of the extractive frontier. It is no coincidence, then, that since 2012–13 the IACHR has been under the magnifying glass of Latin American governments. For example, the Venezuelan government decided to withdraw from the IACHR, accusing it of bias and moral decline. Brazil threatened to do the same, after the IACHR recommended suspending construction of the Belo

Monte mega-dam because it was carried out without due consultation with Indigenous populations.[5]

FPIC tends to encounter an increasingly complex and dynamic field of social and legal dispute. From the perspective of Latin American governments, in times of developmental neoextractivism, FPIC constitutes something more than a stone in their shoe. Beyond the grandiloquent statements made in the name of Indigenous rights and the defence of Pachamama, there is no Latin American government that has not sought to weaken FPIC and make it non-binding through different laws and regulations as well as facilitate authority over the process or manipulation of it in the context of a large power imbalance. This is the case not only for authoritarian governments that continue to toe the neoliberal line but also for progressive governments such as the one headed by Evo Morales, who did not hesitate to manipulate use of FPIC during the Tipnis conflict. The same went for the progressive but anti-Indigenous government of Rafael Correa in Ecuador, which, despite ratifying the principle of FPIC in the country's constitution, in practice did not fulfil its provisions. As for Peru, a succession of neoliberal regimes, from Alan García to Ollanta Humala, sought to put a (violent) brake on the demand for the right to consultation, trying to limit it to the peoples of the Amazonian forests to the detriment of the Andean communities, many of which oppose the installation of mega-mining projects. The effort to limit the application of FPIC also occurred in Argentina under the progressive regime of the Kirchners, which implemented various strategic laws regarding the exploitation of natural resources (such as the 2014 hydrocarbons law, which includes fracking) without requiring companies and governments to consult with Indigenous Peoples.

In March 2015, the Bolivian government, replacing all previous regulations, modified the rules for participation and consultation regarding fossil fuel projects. A decree in May of the same year opened up protected areas to exploration for oil and gas. Likewise, according to the Documentation and Information Centre of Bolivia, over seven years there were at least forty-nine projects with prior consultation but without any environmental evaluation, which meant that the affected populations were unaware of the environmental impacts of these activities in their territory.[6] The so-called Patriotic Agenda 2025 involves different territories and even protected areas where Indigenous communities are settled. Even the right to prior consultation has been distorted to speed up execution of oil investments (Gandarillas 2014: 123).

FPIC has turned out to be one of the most difficult and controversial issues for international, regional and national regulations regarding the rights of Indigenous Peoples. Although it is a "specialized instrument," in only two decades it has been subject to many conflicts where large economic interests, as well as the survival of Indigenous Peoples and other ethnic groups, are involved. Indigenous Peoples find themselves in a situation of contrasts and contradictions. The recognition of collective rights opens up numerous debates in Latin America about the processes of pluralist democratization in the twenty-first century and, especially, the viability and scope of said rights enunciated at the international level and contained in all political constitutions currently in force in Latin America. So we are facing a dilemma that accounts for the collision between two dynamics. On the one hand, since the middle of the twentieth century, we have witnessed the global expansion of the frontier of Indigenous Peoples' cultural and political rights. Concepts such as territorial autonomy, collective rights and the plurinational state inform the indigenist narrative and illustrate the growing political empowerment of Indigenous Peoples in different countries of Latin America. On the other hand, the vertiginous expansion of the frontier of extractive capital accounts for a new process of boxing Indigenous Peoples into an ever-reduced territory, which threatens the preservation of their basic life resources. "Dispossession" and "recolonization" are some of the terms used recurrently by numerous Indigenous spokespeople as well as social movements. In short, the expansion of the extractive frontier impedes the possibility of applying the collective rights of Indigenous Peoples at global, national and local levels.

Popular Forms of Feminism in the South

Historically, the role of women in social struggles in the Global South has been very important. In recent decades in Latin America, women have become even more prominent: Indigenous women, peasants, Afro-descendants, poor rural and urban women, lesbians and trans women have emerged out of the silence and mobilized, re-creating relationships of solidarity and new forms of collective self-management. To account for this empowerment, there is more and more talk about forms of popular feminism, which, beyond their differences, are associated with the most marginalized sectors and tend to question the individualist and modern Western vision of society, development and the future in favour of a greater appreciation of the "collective and community experience" (Korol 2016).

Among the possible forms of popular feminism in the region, what stand out are types of *communitarian feminism*, which highlight the existence of forms of modernity that differ from the dominant Western one and link decolonization with dismantlement of the patriarchy. Within this camp are feminist groups that link patriarchy with colonial history, and others that, far from any idealization of community, emphasize its "refurbishment" (Lorena Cabnal, Xinka feminist in Guatemela) or "colonial intersection" (a double patriarchy including that which already existed and that which came with the white man; Julieta Paredes, Aymara feminist of the Asamblea Feminista Comunitaria in Bolivia) within the framework of existing peasant-Indigenous communities.

In tune with this empowerment, as socioenvironmental conflicts have expanded, Latin American women have acquired a growing role at the forefront of resistance. In the case of Argentina, the group Mothers of Ituzaingó Neighbourhood in the city of Córdoba was a pioneer in denouncing the impacts of glyphosate on health, which led to the first criminal trial on this issue in Argentina (Svampa and Viale 2014). Another development of note is the persistence of the women who were part of the local assemblies of Chilecito and Famatina (teachers, housewives, merchants), which resisted the attack of mining corporations, even expelling four companies (including Canadian giant Barrick Gold) from 2005 to 2009. Finally, the resistance of Mapuche women against fracking in Neuquén must also be noted, in particular the efforts of Cristina Lincopan, now deceased, and Relmu Ñamku, who in 2015 had to face a trial for attempted homicide in relation to a rock-throwing incident during a Mapuche protest against land dispossession. In Chile, there is the case of the Women of Zones of Sacrifice in Resistance of Quintero-Puchuncaví, who oppose environmental contamination in an industrial area near the city of Valparaíso, a phenomenon analyzed by Paola Bolados and Alejandra Sánchez Cuevas (2017) in terms of feminist political ecology and environmental violence.

The same resistance of women in the face of an expanding oil frontier can be found in Colombia (Roa-Avendaño, Roa-García, Chaparro, Camacho et al. 2017). These are just some examples, but the fact is that women play a central role in the ecoterritorial struggles happening in all the countries of the region. It is about individual and at the same time collective voices. Listening carefully to them helps us understand different levels of thought and action, because behind each grievance and testimony it is possible to see the specific struggles of women— struggles that involve a strong identification with the land and its vital cycles of reproduction, as well as the demystification of the myth of development and the construction of a different relationship with nature. From the public to the private, we can see the demand for a free, honest voice, "our own voice" (Gilligan 2015), that questions patriarchy in all its dimensions and seeks to relocate the ethics of care in a central and liberating place indisputably associated with the human condition. Certainly, the evolving nature of the struggles entails a questioning of patriarchy, a model of domination of one gender over another, a binary and hierarchical matrix that separates and privileges the masculine over the feminine.

In other words, the struggles of women — engaged in Indigenous and peasant organizations, socioenvironmental movements, environmental NGOs and cultural collectives — are building a different relationship between society and nature, a relationship in which human beings are not understood as entities outside of nature but rather as part of it. At the heart of this relational vision is the notion of interdependency, reinterpreted as ecodependence, which presents an understanding of human reality through recognition and care of others and nature.

In short, several authors refer to the growing importance of forms of feminism in the South, among them Vandana Shiva, who often talks about the "ecofeminism of survival" in regards to the diverse experiences of women in the defence of health, survival and territory, which has led to an awareness of the strong connections between women and environmentalism, feminism and ecology. Along this line, it is interesting to explore the links between Southern forms of popular feminism and the ecofeminist perspective. Although the term "ecofeminist" was born in the 1970s and numerous authors work in this field, it is in recent years that their contributions have been widely disseminated. Ecofeminism takes up the diagnosis of the ecological crisis, which it understands as a social crisis of an anthropological character, the product of humans' double domination in terms of interpersonal relationships and relationships with nature. Ecofeminism has a similar interpretation of the relationship between one gender and another, a relationship that is expressed through a logic of identity that justifies the devaluation and marginalization of those considered different: women with respect to men, and the natural with respect to the human.

Finally, it is worth mentioning that there are different currents within ecofeminism, including differentialist or identity feminism, which naturalizes the relationship between women and nature, and constructivist ecofeminism,[7] which conceives of this relationship as a sociohistorical construction linked to the sexual division of labour. From my perspective, it is important not to fall into an essentialist vision of the woman-nature relationship, because the key is still the field of elective affinities posed by the exploitation of the unequal division of work and the separation between the production and reproduction of the social sphere. However, it must be said that in Latin America, there is a significant presence of popular and communitarian forms of feminism of a spiritualist nature, which contain certain elements of the essentialist perspective "but without demonizing the male" (Puleo 2011), and which, above all, emphasize identification with the land and the defence of life cycles.

NOTES

1. <http://www.olca.cl/oca/justicia/justicia02.htm>.
2. The report dates from 2014 and the mapping was done by the Support Project for the Special Rapporteur on the rights of Indigenous Peoples of the University of Arizona. The other "problematic knots" or nodal points of conflict include the inadequate or nonexistent legal safeguards of the rights of Indigenous Peoples over their lands, waters, natural resources, biodiversity and territory; conflicts over affected sacred places; the nonexistent or deficient independent evaluation of environmental, economic and territorial impacts of extractive projects; and exclusion of Indigenous Peoples from benefit-sharing due to exploitation of resources in their territories — in short, the criminalization of social protest by Indigenous Peoples against projects that affect their rights and territories (CEPAL 2014: 58).
3. Compañía General de Combustibles "continued to blast open the forest to build new roads using pentolite — one of the world's three most powerful listed explosives due to its detonation velocity — resulting in deforestation and destruction of trees and plants of sacred and cultural value to the community" (Centre for Justice and International Law n.d.).
4. <www.corteidh.or.cr/docs/casos/articulos/seriec_245_esp.pdf>.
5. In recent years, the IACHR has been criticized for the politicization of its sentences. It has had numerous conflicts with Venezuela (complaints of violation of human rights), Ecuador (complaints of violation of freedom of the press) and Nicaragua (complaints of violation of human rights and lack of rights of Nicaraguans working in Costa Rica). Also, it has been reproached for never condemning any dictator or Latin American dictatorship, something that happened, for example, after the coup against Manuel Zelaya in Honduras.
6. Because of this, conflicts persist in eighteen Indigenous territories and eleven protected areas. According to the government, environmental impact assessment is not tied to the need for prior consultation.
7. See Aguinaga, Lang, Mokrani and Santillana (2013) and Daza-Quintanilla, Ruiz-Alba and Ruiz-Navarro (2013), who have examined popular feminism in Peru, linking it to ecofeminism. In the case of Argentina, the role of women in socioenvironmental movements has been analyzed from the perspective of ecofeminism in a pioneering way by Bilder (2013).

REFERENCES

Acosta, Alberto. 2011. "Los derechos de la naturaleza. Una lectura sobre el derecho a la existencia." In A. Acosta and E. Martínez (eds.), *La Naturaleza con Derechos.* Quito, Ecuador: Abya Yala.

Acselard, Henri (ed.). 2004. *Conflitos ambientais no Brasil.* Río de Janeiro: Relume Dumará-Fundaçao Heinrich BoÃàll.

Aguinaga, Margarita, Miriam Lang, Dunia Mokrani and Alejandra Santillana. 2013. "Critiques and Alternatives to Development: A Feminist Perspective." In M. Lang and D. Mokrani (eds.), *Beyond Development: Alternative Visions from Latin America.* Amsterdam, The Netherlands: Transnational Institute and Rosa Luxembourg Foundation.

Bilder, Marisa. 2013. *Las mujeres como sujetos políticos en las luchas contra la megaminería en Argentina. Registros acerca de la deconstrucción de dualismos en torno a la Naturaleza y al género.* Trabajo de Maestría, Barcelona: Universitat Jaume I.

Bolados, Paola, and Alejandra Sánchez Cuevas. 2017. "Una ecología política feminista en construcción: El caso de las 'mujeres de zonas de sacrificio en resistencia,' Región de Valparaíso, Chile." *Psicoperspectivas,* 16, 2: 33–42. doi: 10.5027/psicoperspectivas-vol16-issue2-fulltext-977.

Centre for Justice and International Law. n.d. "Sarayaku: In Defense of Territory." <https://www.arcgis.com/apps/MapJournal/index.html?appid=e96a01a0426344cdb08d67e0408b24d0>.

CEPAL. 2014. *Anuario Estadístico de América Latina y el Caribe.* Santiago de Chile: CEPAL.

Daza-Quintanilla, Mar, Nadia Ruiz-Alba and Clara Ruiz-Navarro. 2013. "Pistas y aportes de los ecofeminismos en el Perú." In Raphael Hoetmer, Miguel Castro and José de Echave Mar

Daza (eds.), *Minería y Movimientos sociales en el Perú. Instrumentos y propuestas para la defensa de la vida, el agua y los territorios.* Lima: Cooper-acción-PDGT.

Esteva, Gustavo. 2007. "Commons: Más allá de los conceptos de bien, derecho humano y propiedad,' Entrevista con Gustavo Esteva sobre el abordaje y la gestión de los bienes comunes." Entre realizada por Anne Becker en el marco de la Conferencia Internacional sobre Ciudadanía y Comunes, México, diciembre.

Gandarillas, Marcos. 2014. "Bolivia: La década dorada del extractivismo." En *Extractivismo: nuevos contextos de dominación y resistencia.* Cochabamba: CEDIB.

Gilligan, Carol. 2015. *La ética del cuidado.* Barcelona: Cuadernos de la Fundación Víctor Grífols i Lucas. <http://www.secpal.com/%5cdocumentos%5cblog%5CCuaderno30.pdf>.

Gudynas, Eduardo. 2009. "La ecología política del giro biocéntrico en la nueva Constitución del Ecuador." *Revista de Estudios Sociales,* 32: 34–47.

Korol, Claudia (ed.). 2016. *Feminismos populares: Pedagogías y Políticas.* Buenos Aires: América Libre-El Colectivo.

Lang, Miriam, and Dunia Mokrani (eds.). 2013. *Beyond Development: Alternative Visions from Latin America.* Amsterdam, The Netherlands, Transnational Institute and Rosa Luxembourg Foundation.

Puleo, Alicia. 2011. "Ecofeminismo para otro mundo posible." <http://www.

mujeresenred.net/spip.php?article1921>.

Roa-Avendaño, Tatiana, María Cecilia Roa-García, Jessica Toloza Chaparro, Luisa María Navas Camacho et al. 2017. *Como el agua y el aceite. Conflictos socioambientales por la extracción petrolera.* Bogotá: Censat-Agua Viva. <https://www.slideshare.net/delDespojoCrnicas/como-el-agua-y-el-aceite-conflictos-socioambientales-por-la-extraccin-de-petrleo-76484130>.

Rodríguez Garavito, César. 2012. "El derecho en los campos minados." In *Etnicidad. gov: los recursos naturales, los pueblos indígenas y el derecho a la consulta previa en los campos sociales minados*, 8–24. Bogotá: Dejusticia.

Svampa, Maristella, and E. Viale. 2014. *Maldesarrollo. La Argentina del extractivismo y el despojo.* Buenos Aires: Editorial Katz.

4 Towards Neoextractivism in Extremis

I n this chapter I explore some of the extreme manifestations of the current neoextractive phase of capitalist development, which include, among other things, an increase in state and parastatal repression as seen in the murder of environmental activists, the emergence of new criminal territorialities linked to illegal mining, reinforcement of the patriarchal structure in a context of masculinization and, finally, the expansion of extreme energy. Also, to complement this reading geopolitically, the last section looks at the expansion of extraction in countries at the centre of the world system.

The Advance of Extractive Violence

The 2008–10 period of the current phase of capitalist development in Latin America — the second half of the commodities boom and the progressive cycle —witnessed a multiplication of extractive projects, as reflected in the various national development plans and electoral platforms of the different presidents that assumed power. From the "mining and energy locomotive" of Colombia's Manuel Santos (Plan Nacional del Desarrollo 2010–14), through Argentina's Cristina Fernández de Kirchner (Agri-food Strategic Program 2020) and Venezuela's Hugo Chávez (the Orinoco Mining Arc, first formulated as a development plan and later reformulated by Nicolás Maduro), to Bolivia's Evo Morales (the passage of the "great industrial leap" in 2010 and the Patriotic Agenda in 2015), in each case the government bet its national development strategy on an exponential increase in the number and scale of extractive megaprojects, promoting the indiscriminate exploitation of natural resources with the aim of exporting them in primary commodity form to meet growing demand.

The other side of this process was an increase in conflict, which contributed directly or indirectly to the criminalization of socioenvironmental struggles and an increase in state and parastatal violence. According to Global Witness (2014), from 2002 to 2013 there were 908 documented killings of environmental activists around the world, of which 83.7 percent (760 cases) took place in Latin America. The data also show that an increase occurred in 2007 and again in 2009 — that is, coinciding with the proliferation of extractive projects, as reflected in the development programs presented by the different governments.

At the beginning of 2012, Panama registered strong episodes of repression that cost the lives of two members of the Ngäbe-Buglé Indigenous community. In Peru during the government of Ollanta Humala (2011–16), twenty-five people died in a context of repression, mainly in the Cajamarca region, where villagers mobilized against the Conga mining project. In 2015, after Brazil (fifty deaths) and the Philippines (thirty-three deaths), Colombia came third in terms of deaths, with twenty-six murders of environmental defenders and activists. In March 2016, Berta Cáceres of COPINH was murdered by repressive forces in Honduras for opposing a hydroelectric dam.[1] In January 2017, the feminist and anti-mega-mining activist Laura Vásquez Pineda, a member of the Committee for the Defence of Life and Peace in Guatemala, was murdered. Likewise, in Argentina under the right-wing regime and conservative government of Mauricio Macri and in the context of a hardening dispute over land, Rafael Nahuel, of Mapuche origin, was shot and killed by police, and another young man, Santiago Maldonado, died by drowning in a situation of state repression.[2]

Neoextractivism is taking more and more victims in the globalized periphery, with Latin America leading the way. As in other times, the illusion of El Dorado is being renewed through a dialectic of dispossession and dependence that is accompanied by more extractivism, more violence and, therefore, less democracy. This process has been intensifying. Just in 2016, of two hundred murders of environmental activists, 60 percent took place in Latin America. This statistic was replicated in 2017.[3] Nothing indicates that these indexes will improve; quite the contrary, if we take into account the current turn to the far right illustrated by countries such as Argentina and Brazil, whose current governments have not only deepened the extractivist model in all its versions, accentuating the state violence perpetrated against the most vulnerable populations, but also enacted a series of public policies that involve a significant regression in terms of social rights.

Enclaves and Criminal Territorialities

Enclave economies associated with extractivism have a long history in the region, beginning with the extraction of minerals and the export of different raw materials (sugar cane, guano, rubber, wood, among others). Company towns, which sometimes become cities, know about the overnight splendour and waste, poverty and extreme wealth. But when the lights finally go out, and capital retires to continue its looting and dispossession elsewhere, it leaves behind a degraded territory, a zone of sacrifice and a legacy of environmental and sociohealth impacts for local communities. This cycle of capital is marked by the expansion of the commodities frontier, a historical-geographical model based on rapid appropriation (Moore 2013); once a resource is exhausted, capital seeks to expand and diversify geographically.

At the beginning of the twentieth century, enclave economies were replaced by regional economies, which were mainly linked to the oil industry and in the hands of the state, through nationalization processes that occurred in Latin America during the 1940s and 1950s and led to a new phase based on sovereignty projects. In the current era, mining neoextractivism and increasingly the oil tanker seem to take up the most classic route of the export enclave associated with accelerated accumulation and expansion of the exploitation frontier. In social terms, the configuration of extractive territories translates into the dislocation of the previous economic and social fabric, and consolidation of a strong structure of inequalities that includes different aspects linked to style and quality of life, to labour relations and gender. The association between export enclaves and extraordinary profits leads to a significant increase in the cost of living, which accentuates wage disparities between oil workers and miners, who receive high wages, and the rest of the population. The oil and mining boom also brings high rents and a housing crisis. Finally, social disintegration and the peculiarities of oil work generate social problems such as addiction to drugs, alcohol and gambling. There is an abundant bibliography about this subject, and I examined this topic in Svampa and Viale (2014). In fact, extractive territories usually take a different shape than non-extractive territories, in that they tend to enhance and extend already existing social problems such as wage disparities, high prices, addictions, crime and prostitution — and more recently drug trafficking and the expansion of criminal networks.

The new century saw diverse changes at the national and global levels. The social disorganization that societies are experiencing has produced notable changes in the social fabric and accentuated and diversified forms of collective violence. Today's societies are much more fragmented, with the explosion of drug trafficking, the persistence of inequalities and marginalization and the growing problem of insecurity. The amplification of these chains of violence[4] finds fertile ground in extractive contexts through new criminal territorialities, where marginality and collusion vis-à-vis the central state combine with predatory extractivism in the search for windfall profits.

This phenomenon is registered today in certain marginal regions of Venezuela where the extractive frontier is expanding (Terán 2016). Keep in mind that as of 2013, with the end of the so-called commodities supercycle, several governments in the region took a new extractivist turn in response to the emergence of trade deficits. As E. Lander notes, the main trigger of the crisis in Venezuela was the drastic fall in the international price of oil.[5] The Maduro government initiated an intensive search for foreign exchange and, in keeping with the 2013–19 Patriotic Plan, in February 2016 created by decree a new National Strategic Zone of Development, the Arco Minero del Orinoco, which opened almost 112,000 square kilometres (12 percent of the national territory) to mega-mining for the exploitation of gold, diamonds, coltan, iron and other minerals. In order to attract foreign investment, the Maduro government signed agreements with 150 national and transnational corporations. Their actual content is unknown because under the current economic emergency decree, these contracts do not require the authorization of the National Assembly. Thus, the expansion of the commodity frontier through mega-mining was presented as a new "magical" way to diversify the economy away from oil extractivism, a project that today is in crisis. According to Terán (2016), this will result in new extractivist mapping, in which "the new appropriation of territory on the extractive frontier would exceed the historical map and expand into the areas of natural reserves, offshore extraction and national parks."

Beyond the megaprojects planned for the Arco Minero del Orinoco, other territorialities in this region illustrate that new extreme forms of extractivism have emerged. Recent research points to the emergence and consolidation of criminal gangs linked to artisanal and illegal mining. The 2016 massacre of twenty-eight miners in Tumeremo, in the state of Bolívar, (Pardo 2016), although not the first such attack, contributed to making visible the growing relationship between rent-seeking, crime and artisanal and illegal mining, a phenomenon that has intensified over the last ten years (Romero and Ruiz 2018).

What is now known as the mining *pranato*[6] reveals the contours of a new violent and mafia-like extractive territoriality, which has as its counterpart a state with weak regulatory capacity and territorial control — and links with armed gangs. Thus, we are facing the emergence from below of a parastatal sphere that involves a large number of legal and illegal economic actors and social subjects. Such criminal structures control not only territories but also population and subjectivities, which is a blow to any attempt to reconstruct a democratic project. And all this is in place even before transnational companies enter the territories with their predatory logic.

The expansion of criminal structures linked to illegal mining is not specific to Venezuela; it can also be found in Peru, for example, where in 2016 criminal organizations enjoyed greater profits than drug trafficking networks.[7] However, the phenomenon in Venezuela assumes more specific and stark features as a result of the crisis of the state and the economic debacle that has resulted in the expulsion of different populations in the search for a new survival strategy. In short, this type of socioterritorial configuration can be read as an extreme form of extractivism characterized by social disorganization, inequality, the pillage of resources and the reinforcement of patriarchal domination, which strengthens already existing chains of violence.

No less serious is the conjunction of political patronage and extractive violence that marks the tortuous relationship between the ostensibly "progressive" Bolivian government led by social movement leader Evo Morales and the powerful mining cooperatives in a dispute over a declining mining surplus as the period of extraordinary profitability comes to an end. The 2016 murder of government deputy minister Rodolfo Illanes by some members of the cooperative sector in retaliation for police repression had a great national and international impact. Without a doubt, it was part of an extractivist war, because what was at stake, in a context of falling international mineral prices, was control of the surplus. Like an apprentice sorcerer, the government had to face an entrepreneurial model of excessive corporatism, which Morales had reinforced through the provision of economic privileges in exchange for political support. It should be clarified that many associations in the cooperative sector are not even cooperatives but covert private companies that outsource labour in conditions of overexploitation, which include extensive working days (up to sixteen hours a day), while selling the extracted product to transnational companies. According to the Documentation and Information Centre of Bolivia there are 100,000 to 120,000 cooperative miners, but an important part of the sector (40 to 50 percent) is subcontracted. Thus, the reality is that a set of owners emerged who were enriched thanks to exploitative labour conditions and high mineral prices during the commodities boom. With the economic bonanza, the number of cooperatives increased from 500 in 2005 to 1,600 by 2015. After gas, mining today represents the second-greatest source of wealth in Bolivia, accounting for 25 percent of exports, which include tin, zinc, silver, copper and gold.

The Other Side of Patriarchy: Extractivism and Chains of Violence

There is a historical relationship between oil and mining activity, the masculinization of territories and the reinforcement of patriarchy. Indeed, where a strong concentration of men is found, prostitution tends to become naturalized — that is, not seen as a social and cultural problem. Further, in a context of the globalization of criminal networks, prostitution and trafficking have increased over recent decades. The trafficking of women for the sex industry generates huge profits in an increasingly globalized crime circuit (Sassen 2003), which involves the complicity and participation of political and judicial powers.

A close relationship is registered throughout Latin America between mining, prostitution and increased trafficking. In countries such as Bolivia, Peru, Colombia and Mexico, trafficking networks are all associated with illegal mining. This is the case, for example, in the Puno region in Bolivia, where thousands of cases of trafficking in women and sexual exploitation have been reported. As Livia Wagner, author of the report *Organized Crime and Illegal Mining in Latin America*, writes, "There is a strong link between illegal mining and sexual exploitation. Whenever there are large migrations of men to an area, there is a great demand for sexual services that often generate sex trafficking" (Miranda 2016). It also happens in the mining areas of Peru, such as the Amazon region of Madre de Dios, where illegal gold extraction can be found. In the case of Argentina, trafficking and prostitution follow oil, mining and soybeans.

Further, there has been an increase in state and parastatal violence against women who oppose neoextractivism. It has already been pointed out that the criminalization of, aggression towards and murder of defenders of the environment have increased notoriously in the region. From 2011 to 2016, human rights organizations registered 1,700 cases of aggression against women environmentalists in South and Central America (Maldonado 2016). The majority of this aggression has been carried out in contexts of forced eviction, where women are physically and sexually abused by police forces or paramilitary groups (Fondo de Acción Urgente-América Latina 2017).

One of the most shocking recent crimes, as mentioned earlier, was the murder of Berta Cáceres of COPINH in Honduras. Another resounding case of persecution and intimidation is that of Peru's Máxima Acuña, a member of the Association of Women in Defence of Life as well as the Latin American Union of Women, who opposes the Conga mining megaproject.[8] There is also the case of Acción Ecológica, an internationally known Ecuadorian

NGO dedicated to research and advice, composed almost exclusively of women. They have experienced at least two attempts over the last decade by the government of Rafael Correa (in 2009 and in 2016) to dissolve the organization because of their struggle in support of the rights of nature and communities in the fight against neoextractivism.

In short, where extractive activities, characterized by the masculinization of territories and making of extraordinary profits, have irrupted, already existing social problems have been intensified or exacerbated. Thus, one consequence has been the accentuation of stereotypes associated with a sexual division of labour, which aggravate gender inequalities and break down the community fabric while facilitating pre-existing chains of violence (Svampa 2017). In a context aggravated by the social, labour and spatial characteristics of an enclave economy, this negatively affects the situation of women. The strong wage disparities between women and men reinforce traditional gender roles (woman-housekeeper-caretaker vs. male-worker-provider). In many countries, women's community and ancestral roles are weakening, since extractive industries tear apart the community fabric and result in the abandonment of rural livelihoods and economic activities and even the forced displacement of a population unable to adapt to the forces of change (Fondo de Acción Urgente-América Latina 2017). In addition, the sexual exploitation of women crystallizes the view of them as sexual objects. These conditions tend to aggravate acts of violence — physical and sexual — against environmental defenders and activists.

In other words, the consolidation of socioterritorial configurations characterized by masculinization and a dismantling of the social fabric reinforces the matrix of patriarchal domination and aggravates the chains of violence. All of this results in a serious setback regarding issues of gender equity and a very dangerous re-enactment of the worst forms of patriarchy linked to sexual slavery.

The Expansion of Extreme Energy and New Conflicts

Technological advances have made it possible to look for other forms of fossil fuel deposits, sometimes referred to as unconventional oil and gas, which are technically more difficult and economically more expensive to extract and also pose greater risks of contamination. Following the definition proposed by Tatiana Roa Avendaño of Censat-Agua Viva from Colombia and Hernán Scandizzo of the Observatorio Petrolero Sur from Argentina, in this book I use the concept of extreme energy, which is broader than unconventional fossil fuels and refers "not only to the characteristics of hydrocarbons, but also to a context in which the exploitation of gas, crude oil and coal entails ever greater geological, environmental, labour and social risks" (Roa-Avendaño and Scandizzo 2017).

There are different types of extreme energy. Shale gas is found in shale deposits, sedimentary rock formed from silt, clay and organic matter at a depth of 1,000 to 5,000 metres. Shale is porous but not very permeable because its pores are very small and not well connected. Another form of extreme energy is tight gas, which is trapped in a compact geological formation such as a sandstone or limestone. There is also coal gas, which is attached to coal at a depth of 500 and 2,000 metres, as well as heavy crude oil or tar sands, which comes with high extraction costs but is currently being extracted in Alberta, Canada, and in the Orinoco belt of Venezuela. Finally, we should not forget the offshore deposits, located in deep waters that are increasingly distant from the coast, which in some cases are extracted after penetrating thick layers of salt. As with the pre-salt oil reserves in Brazil, the depth can reach more than 7,000 metres.

Extreme energy carries high economic costs as well as heavy environmental and sociohealth impacts. Its extraction requires hydraulic fracturing, or fracking,[9] an experimental technique by which it is possible to extract the gas or oil trapped in rocks since time immemorial. This technique involves the high-pressure injection of sand and chemicals into rock formations rich with hydrocarbons, in order to increase their permeability and facilitate the extraction of oil and gas.

The expansion of extreme energy is closely linked to geopolitical decisions made unilaterally by the United States. Towards the year 2000, the United States proposed the strategic objective of lessening its dependence on the oil production of Arab countries and increasing energy self-sufficiency through the exploitation of extreme energy. In order to make this economically viable, oil companies received important concessions from the state, from strong financial incentives to exemptions from compliance with environmental regulations. This happened under the presidency of George Bush in 2005, when Congress approved the Energy Policy Act, which contained the "Halliburton Loophole," named after the corporation that lobbied for it. It exempted the gas industry from the obligation to respect laws designed to protect drinking water and other environmental protection regulations introduced by the Environmental Protection Agency. Further, US companies are protected by confidentiality measures and until recently did not even have to detail which chemicals they used in fracturing liquids.

This decision, driven by the oil lobby and justified in the name of geopolitics, will result in a reconfiguration of the global energy map based on fossil fuels. Over the last ten years, the United States has strengthened its leadership in regard to the production of so-called unconventional fossil fuels, which are now seen as a viable alternative to conventional energy sources, despite their higher economic cost, greater pollution and environmental damage, and lower energy efficiency. It is thought that by the end of 2030 the United States, a net exporter of gas, could also become a net oil exporter, thanks to the utilization of extraction technologies such as fracking. Russia and the Middle East, in this context, like China and other countries, will thus lose their pre-eminent position in the energy sector. A 2017 report from the International Energy Agency estimates that US shale oil production from 2010 to 2025 will increase by eight million barrels per day, which "would match the highest sustained period of oil output growth by a single country in the history of oil markets."

In 2010, the State Department launched the Global Shale Gas Initiative, now known as the Unconventional Gas Technical Engagement Program, focused on fracking. It was a gamble in which Washington invited several countries to discuss the benefits and risks of this technique that, according to its proponents, will radically change the energy market. In April 2011, the Energy Information Administration published a report on the value and location of the main reserves worldwide. Although that study has since been questioned, especially as regards overestimates of gas reserves, it is still used as the basis of an argument for accessing these reserves. According to the study, the largest deposits can be found in China, the United States, Argentina, Mexico, South Africa, Australia, Canada, Libya, Algeria and Brazil. While China and the United States lead in terms of non-conventional gas, with 19.3 percent and 13 percent of worldwide reserves respectively, Argentina and Mexico are located in third and fourth place, with 11.7 percent and 10.3 percent respectively.

Argentina has come to be the fracking beachhead in Latin America. In 2012, in a context of increasing energy shortages, promising estimates as to the size of unconventional oil and gas reserves led the government of Cristina Fernández to a partial renationalization of the company Yacimientos Petrolíferos Fiscales, at that time owned by the Spanish company Repsol. Unconventional fossil fuels in the country are found mostly in northern Patagonia, in the Neuquén basin, which covers an area of about 120,000 square kilometres. Beyond the peak oil crisis, the existence of unconventional fossil fuels unleashed an El Dorado fever, which helped minimize any debate on the environmental and sociohealth risks of fracking. This was strengthened by the nationalist rhetoric of the Kirchner regime, which promoted the passage from a "commodity" paradigm to a "strategic resources" paradigm in the formulation of the government's energy policy. According to Energy Information Administration data, without considering the United States and Canada, Argentina and China led the development of shale gas in 2015. As occurred with soybeans, Argentina has become an open-pit laboratory for the implementation of one of the most controversial hydrocarbon extraction techniques, within a regulatory framework that is increasingly favourable to foreign investment — especially after the signing of an agreement between Yacimientos Petrolíferos Fiscales and Chevron, which was the gateway for large-scale fracking in the country and was followed by other joint venture agreements. But progressivist Kirchner was not alone in this commitment to extreme energy. Centre and right-wing opposition forces supported Kirchner's decision to expand the extractive frontier by means of fracking. Once again, the Commodities Consensus, which projected that Neuquén would be the new Saudi Arabia thanks to Vaca Muerta (the largest shale formation in the country), had managed to unite progressives, conservatives and neoliberals with the same vision of development.

History, however, is not linear. As of 2014, the fall in international oil prices had put a brake on the El Dorado fever in Vaca Muerta. But this did not prevent the start of a process of social and territorial reconfiguration based in Añelo, a town occupied by large transnational companies, where everything is ready to (re)start when the signal is given. It is just a matter of waiting for the international price of oil to rise beyond what large global corporations consider profitable; then the expected investment will come. The policy of the Kirchner government to subsidize oil production continues under the administration of the right-wing authoritarian Mauricio Macri, who in January 2017 relaunched the Vaca Muerta project in its neoliberal El Dorado–inspired version by signing agreements with energy companies that guaranteed labour market flexibility and transferred the cost of accumulation to the weakest sectors of the exploitation chain — the working class.

It should be noted that the Vaca Muerta region is far from being an "empty territory" as conceived by provincial and national authorities. At least twenty Indigenous communities would be directly impacted by fracking and other destructive operations of extractive capital in the region. And Vaca Muerta is not the only territory in Argentina where fracking is done. It is also conducted in the Upper Rio Negro Valley area, where the exploitation of tight gas proceeds among plantations of pears and apples, threatening to displace this type of economy.

In 2014, following protests carried out by the Mapuche Confederation, the government of Neuquén was forced to recognize the community of Campo Maripe, which had been settled in the area since 1927. The Observatorio Petrolero Sur points out that the disputed territory covers 10,000 hectares, but the government recognizes only 900 hectares as part of the community. On such a small piece of land, it is impossible for the Indigenous groups in the area to undertake livestock grazing and agriculture, the two activities that define their livelihoods. This is just one example, as there are many more disputed territories, subject to conflict between the mining companies and agribusinesses encroaching on Indigenous land and the Mapuche communities engaged in a war of active resistance against the diverse modalities of neoextractivism, including the advance of resource-seeking extractive capital and land-grabbing.

As of 2013 in Mexico, the government of Peña Nieto had implemented a program of energy reform, which opened the door to contracts with private investors and placed the issue of exploitation of extreme energy in the form of shale deposits and compact sands on the agenda, with the objective of addressing the fall of national oil production and the importation of natural gas. Several states were committed to this project, including Tampicas, Veracruz and Chihuahua. In addition, there is evidence that fracking had already been used in shale deposits as early as 2010 by Petróleos Mexicanos (Pemex). Official figures recognize the use of fracking in 1,500 active wells, but more recent data provided through research conducted by the CartoCrítica reveals the existence of 5,000 active wells.

In Colombia in mid-2017, the Ministry of the Environment issued a regulation that would allow the start of offshore oil and gas extraction. However, the government does not have a unified position on the issue of fracking. While the Ministry of the Environment proposed to extend studies on the impacts of fracking for another five years, the Ministry of Energy endorsed the immediate use of fracking. The Alianza Colombiana Contra el Fracking maintains that if fracking follows the path of the expansion of the oil frontier, it could pose a very serious risk to several strategic ecosystems, such as the Sumapaz Páramo, the agricultural pantry of Bogota and the largest páramo in the world, and the Páramo de Chingaza, which supplies around 80 percent of the capital's drinking water.

Meanwhile, in Brazil, the neoliberal government of Michel Temer promoted investment in fossil fuel exploration and production through energy reforms carried out in 2016 and 2017. As in other countries, it became optional for the state company, Petrobras, to participate in global oil consortiums engaged in the exploitation of the pre-salt oil reserves. This change reversed the 2010 reforms that had mandated Petrobras to acquire at least a 30 percent share in any consortium focused on the pre-salt oil reserves (Pulso Energético 2017). In 2017, the Minister of Mines and Energy, Fernando Coelho Filho, stressed that with exploitation of pre-salt oil in the coming years, Brazil would once again experience "euphoria," similar to what occurred under the administration of former president Luiz Inácio Lula da Silva with the discovery of large offshore reserves.

The advance of fracking has generated popular resistance in local communities throughout the continent. Citizens' assemblies, Indigenous communities and peasant women, environmental NGOs, networks of activist scholars and academics, and some unions are at the heart of this resistance. As of 2012 in Argentina, numerous citizens' assemblies and networks had been created to push for a moratorium or prohibition on fracking. By the end of 2017, about fifty towns had ordinances that forbade fracking. In Brazil in 2016, seventy-two cities prohibited fracking, and other data indicate that two hundred fracking-free municipalities and several states are considering prohibition. Many Brazilian activists travel to Argentina to observe in situ the damage caused by extracting this type of extreme energy, especially in the Upper Rio Negro Valley. At a regional level, the Latin American Alliance Against Fracking was created. This network of organizations seeks to promote debate by analyzing the energy context of each country; public policies that promote and regulate fracking; the sociohealth, environmental and economic effects of fracking; the impact of fracking as a model of territorial occupation; and the strategies of mobilization and resistance deployed in each country.

Thus far, the only country in the region that has legislated a moratorium on fracking is Uruguay. In August 2017, environmental groups from Uruguay, Argentina and Brazil marched through northwest Uruguay to demonstrate against fracking, with the protection of the Guaraní aquifer, one of the largest freshwater reserves on the planet, as the banner issue to rally the cause. The moratorium finally became law in December 2017.

Extending the Geography of Extraction

The deepening of neoextractivism and the emergence of extreme forms of it particularly affect countries in the Global South, reconfiguring territories and the frontier of neoextractivism, generating new forms of domination and strengthening the geopolitics of dispossession in a context increasingly marked by state and parastatal repression as well as patriarchal violence. However, the pressure to expand the energy frontier is clearly not limited to the Global South, and a territorial extractive dynamic can be detected in the Global North. A telling example of this is the vertiginous expansion of the oil and energy frontier through exploitation of unconventional oil and gas. Fracking deepens the current energy matrix, which is based on fossil fuels, and consequently poses a strong setback in terms of alternative scenarios and a transition to clean and renewable energy.

It has already been said that the United States decided upon the fracking route in the name of energy self-sufficiency and hydrocarbon sovereignty. The history of its development and the series of environmental and economic exemptions it required, along with the crucial role of the powerful oil lobby, are among the most sordid pages of recent American politics — amplified many times over by the ascension of Donald Trump to the office of president. Since 2000, fracking has transformed the energy reality of the United States, giving it greater autonomy with respect to imports while also making it a place where the true impacts of fracking can be seen: contamination of aquifers, damage to the health of people and animals, earthquakes, higher emissions of methane gas and so on.

The controversial character of fracking can be illustrated though a global mapping of the conflict, which started in the heart of the Imperial North, as reflected by Vermont's ban and moratoriums in cities such as New York and Los Angeles. In Canada, resistance led to its prohibition in Quebec, while in British Columbia urban and Indigenous resistance has formed, following the proposal of a 1,100 kilometre pipeline that would transport bitumen west from Alberta across numerous waterways, communities and Indigenous territories as well as a provincial boundary. In Alberta — home to the town of Fort McMurray, epicentre of the Canadian oil industry — oil and pipeline spills and damage produced by fracking are incalculable, and a desolate landscape covers more than 90,000 square metres of land and water contaminated by the extraction of tar sands, the most dirty fossil fuel. Since 2000, the exploitation of this area has included global corporations such as Chevron, Esson, Total, PetroChina and others.

In Europe, as happened in other places, the reports of the US Department of Energy tended to feed the expectations of a new El Dorado, and not a few countries fell prisoner to this seductive discourse. Perhaps the most dramatic case is Poland, where US companies made their bid in 2011. One of the main lobbyists for this project was Hillary Clinton, then an official of the Barack Obama government. The US government predicted that shale gas reserves in Poland were abundant enough to supply that country with energy for the next three centuries, but four years later the reality ended up being quite different: the cost of extraction and the poor accessibility of deposits led to a reduction in the number of shale gas licences, leading oil companies, including Chevron, to leave the country.

In 2011, France became the first country to prohibit fracking, after resistance from various small towns in the Pyrenees — which was accompanied by an emblematic reference to the José Bové alter-globalization movement[10] (Svampa 2018). Bulgaria followed suit in 2012, while other countries pushed for a moratorium. This was the case, for example, in Germany, one of the countries that most decidedly embarked on a path to transition towards renewable energy. Fracking was also banned in Wales, Ireland and Scotland. In the latter, a consultation in October 2017 resulted in 99 percent of respondents being against fracking for environmental reasons and for the lack of economic benefits. In Spain, the relationship between the central government and resistance to fracking was, and continues to be, very intense. In several communities, such as Cantabria and the Basque Country, elected representatives from the Popular Party supported antifracking laws. Towards 2016, in the face of resistance and an initiative promoted by several parties to prohibit fracking, several oil companies interested in exploiting unconventional oil and gas in Spain opted to abandon the project.

A country that presents a very conflictive scenario is England. According to the British Geological Survey, Great Britain is settled on shale gas fields that could supply the country for some twenty-five years. The first oil and gas drilling of shale here occurred in 2011 and resulted in seismic movements in Blackpool, which led to the first national moratorium. However, the moratorium was lifted some time later by David Cameron's government, which promised tax benefits to municipalities that accepted fracking and proposed to allow it even in protected natural areas. Although it has a lower profile, the British government's approach is not far from Donald Trump's denialism. For example, Prime Minister Theresa May decided to push fracking and nuclear energy while disbanding the Department of Energy and Climate Change.

Thus, the change of the rules of the game by the United States, in its search for energy independence, reconfigured the global board, promoting a kind of deepening of the fossil fuel energy model. So much so that in the beginning, not even the European Union could escape the siren song of fracking, and many countries did not hesitate to sacrifice their territories in the name of and with the promise of energy independence. However, in many of these countries the different governments and the oil lobby met with unexpected resistance, which forced a reconsideration of the cost-benefit relationship not only in economic terms[11] but also in political and social terms.

In short, social resistance in the Global South has been widening and deepening along with the geography of extraction. Meanwhile, in the North, new disputes over natural resources in both Canada and the United States have featured the active resistance of Indigenous communities, while other cases, such as England and France, feature the active resistance of small local communities to the advance of extractive capital, especially in its extreme form (fracking, etc.). Thus, the dilemma posed by the advance and dynamics of extractive capital is not exclusive to the peripheral countries, although it has an undeniably colonial dimension as shown by the paradigmatic case of Latin America.

NOTES

1. In 2015, Berta Cáceres received the Goldman Prize, also known as the Nobel Green Prize, in recognition of her struggle. Cáceres had founded COPINH, which succeeded in forcing the withdrawal of the largest hydroelectric construction company in the world — the Chinese company Synohydro — from the project to construct a dam on the Gualcarque River.
2. Since the beginning of the Macri government, there have been numerous conflicts with the Mapuche people, and Mapuche leaders have been prosecuted.
3. <https://www.theguardian.com/environment/ng-interactive/2017/jul/13/the-defenders-tracker> <http://www.jornada.unam.mx/ultimas/2018/02/02/asesinan-acerca-de-200-defensores-del-medio-ambiente-en-2017-global-witness-5318.html>.
4. The book *La violencia en los márgenes*, written by Javier Auyero and Fernanda Berti (2013), introduces the concept of "chains of violence" — "a series of intersecting circles, through which communication is established between the different types of violence: criminal, interpersonal, domestic and gender." From my perspective, these chains of violence that the authors analyze as part of everyday life in the more neglected neighbourhoods can be seen in society as a whole. The inability of the state to provide a satisfactory and democratic response to the problems generated by these chains of violence not only reflects a capitalist culture of incessant accumulation in contexts of exploitation, exclusion, dispossession and submission but also reveals a worrying democratic regression and even a danger of fascist tendencies in certain sectors of society.
5. See the call launched in April 2016 to stop the ecocide in the Orinoco Mining Arc at <https://entitleblog.org/2016/04/18/called-to-adhesiones-detener-el-ecocidio-minero-en-la-basin-of-orinoco-venezuela/>.
6. In prison jargon, "pran" means chief. It may come from a Spanish acronym drawn from words meaning "born serial killer prisoner."
7. *La República*, 2017.
8. For a survey of the process of criminalization and murder of women warriors, see Oxfam (2014).
9. It is only with technological advances and the imminence of the exhaustion of conventional hydrocarbons that the so-called unconventional fossil fuels began to be seen as a viable alternative. Likewise, although hydraulic fracturing technology

has been used for over sixty years to extract oil, it is only over the last two decades that it has been used intensively and on a large scale. See Bertinat, d'Elia, Ochandio, Svampa and Viale (2014) and Svampa and Viale (2014), and Svampa (2018).

10. Bové is one of the founders of the Peasant Confederation in France and an outstanding leader of Via Campesina. He has been part of the alter-globalization movement since the late 1990s. One of his causes was against genetically modified organisms, bringing him into confrontation with large agri-food corporations. In 2007 Bové was presented as a candidate for president of the republic by a left front but received barely 1.32 percent of the vote. Two years later he was elected to the European Parliament and resided in Brussels. Even then he remained dedicated to breeding animals, especially sheep, for the manufacture and direct sale of cheeses, milk and yogurt, in Montredon, located in the department of Aveyron, on the Larzac plateau. In France the fight against fracking began in the adopted homeland of Bové. In 2010 a small town of seven hundred inhabitants called Nan, on the Larzac plateau, found that it was sitting on a huge unconventional gas field and that the French government had already authorized exploration by several oil companies, including Total and GDF Suez. Bové did not hesitate to get involved in this new conflict, coming and going from Brussels. The mobilization expanded to other locations in the region threatened by fracking, and the pressure on the national government grew. Fracking thus became a subject of public debate, and the discussion did not leave anyone indifferent. Hundreds of articles were published in newspapers as well as in large-circulation magazines. A moratorium on fracking was declared in 2011, and it was prohibited in France in 2012. See Svampa (2018).

11. A recent article in the *Wall Street Journal* says that companies that do fracking in the United States have grossly inflated their well yields. They are losing a lot of money and have to keep investing so that current production levels do not fall, despite an adverse international price context, which raises "questions about the strength and profitability of the fracking boom that turned the U.S. into an oil superpower." The article analyzes sixteen thousand wells in North Dakota and Texas, where the Permian Basin is located (Aizen 2019).

REFERENCES

Aizen, Marina. 2019. "El Wall Street Journal las dudas sobre el fracking." April 4.
    <https://www.clarin.com/opinion/hijo-bobo-cambiemos_0_LBfR-9veS.html>.
Auyero, Javier, and María Fernanda Berti. 2013. *La violencia en los márgenes*. Buenos
    Aires: Editorial Katz.
Bertinat, Pablo, Eduardo d'Elia, Roberto Ochandio, Maristella Svampa and Enrique
    Viale. 2014. *20 mitos y realidades del fracking*. Buenos Aires: El Colectivo.
Energy Information Administration. 2011. *World Shale Gas Resources: An Initial
    Assessment of 14 Regions Outside the United States*. <www.eia.gov/cfapps/
    ipdbproject/IEDIndex3.cfm>.
Energy Information Administration. 2013. *Technically Recoverable Shale Oil and Shale
    Gas Resources: An Assessment of 137 Shale Formations in 41 Countries Outside
    the United States*. <https://www.eia.gov/analysis/studies/worldshalegas/pdf/

overview.pdf>.

Fondo de Acción Urgente-América Latina. 2017. *Extractivismo en América Latina y su impacto en la vida de las mujeres.* Colombia: FAU-AL.

Global Witness. 2014. "Deadly Environment." April 15. <https://www.globalwitness. org/documents/12993/deadly%20environment.pdf>.

International Energy Agency. 2017. *World Energy Outlook 2017.* <www.iea.org/ weo2017/>.

La República. April 25, 2017. "They earned 2.6 billion dollars for the production and sale of illegally obtained gold, while the networks dedicated to drug trafficking derived profits from 500 million to a billion dollars." <http://larepublica. pe/sociedad/1035115-mineria-ilegal-genero-more-profits-than-the-drug-trafficking>.

Maldonado, Angel. 2016. "Editorial." *Boletín Reinventerra.*

Miranda, Boris. 2016. "La 'escalofriante' alianza entre la minería ilegal y la explotación sexual en Sudamérica." BBC Mundo, April 12. <http://www.bbc.com/mundo/ noticias/2016/04/160406_ america_latina_alianza_siniestra_mineria_ilegal_ trata_mujeres_prostitucion_sexual_bm>.

Moore, J.W. 2013. "El auge de la ecología-mundo capitalista (ii): las fronteras mercantiles en el auge y decadencia de la apropiación máxima." *Filosofía, política y economía en el Laberinto,* 39: 21–30.

Oxfam. 2014. "Las mujeres rurales de América Latina son luchadoras, no criminales." <https://www.oxfam.org/es/crece-peru-mexico-el-salvador-guatemala-bolivia/ las-mujeres-rurales-de-america-latina-son-luchadoras

Pardo, Daniel. 2016. "Lo que se sabe de la supuesta masacre de 28 mineros en Venezuela." *BBC Mundo.* <http://www.bbc.com/mundo/ noticias/2016/03/160307_venezuela_mineros_tumeremo_dp>.

Pulso Energético. 2017. "La reforma energética en Brasil." October 2. <https:// pulsoenergetico.org/la-reforma-energetica-de-brasil>.

Roa-Avendaño, Tatiana, and Hernán Scandizzo. 2017. "Qué entendemos por energía extrema." In *Extremas. Nuevas fronteras del extractivismo energético en Latinoamérica.* Colombia: Oilwatch Latinoamérica.

Romero, César, and Francisco Ruiz. 2018. "Dinámica de la minería a pequeña escala como sistema emergente." In K. Gabbert and Alexandra Martínez (eds.), *Venezuela desde adentro. Ocho investigaciones para un debate necesario.* Quito: Fundación Rosa Luxemburgo.

Sassen, Saskia. 2003. *Contrageografías de la globalización. Género y ciudadanía en los circuitos fronterizos.* Madrid: Mapas-Traficantes de sueños.

Svampa, Maristella. 2017. *Del cambio de época al fin de ciclo. Gobiernos Progresistas, extractivismo y movimientos sociales.* Buenos Aires: Edhasa.

Svampa, Maristella, and E. Viale. 2014. *Maldesarrollo. La Argentina del extractivismo y el despojo.* Buenos Aires: Editorial Katz.

Svampa, Maristella. 2018. *Chacra 51. Regreso a la Patagonia en los tiempos del fracking.* Buenos Aires: Sudamericana.

Terán Mantovani, Emiliano. 2016. "Las nuevas fronteras de las commodities en Venezuela: extractivismo, crisis histórica y disputas territoriales." *Ciencia Política,* 11, 21: 251–285.

5 The End of the Commodities Boom and the Progressive Cycle, and the Creation of New Dependencies

This chapter explores the geopolitical context, including the global rise of China and the increase of trade with Latin America. It looks at the forms assumed by the new dependency on China, in the light of a truncated Latin American integration, or, rather, a failed autonomous regionalism, which was proposed by the progressive governments. In this line, in the two final sections I reflect on the limits of the progressive cycle.

China and the Frame of a New Dependency

In recent years, trade between Latin America and China has intensified markedly. Heading into the year 2000, China did not occupy a privileged place as a destination for exports or as an origin of imports for the countries of the region. By 2013, though, it had become the top source of imports into Brazil, Paraguay and Uruguay; the second-highest source in the case of Argentina, Chile, Colombia, Costa Rica, Ecuador, Honduras, Mexico, Panama, Peru and Venezuela; and the third-highest source for Bolivia, Nicaragua, El Salvador and Guatemala. In this way, it was displacing the United States, European Union countries and Japan as commercial partners of the region.

In the case of exports from Latin America, China is the first destination for Brazil and Chile, and the second for Argentina, Colombia, Peru, Uruguay and Venezuela (Svampa and Slipak 2018). This exchange is asymmetrical — while 84 percent of exports from Latin American countries to China are commodities, 63.4 percent of Chinese imports into the region are manufactured goods. To mention a few cases, Argentina basically exports soybeans, oleaginous fruits and vegetable oils; Chile, copper; Brazil, soybeans and iron ore; Venezuela and Ecuador, oil; and Peru, iron ore and other minerals (Svampa and Slipak 2018). Even the relationship that a country such as Brazil has with China is very uneven and, as already noted, has been read as a case of "early deindustrialization" due to the inability of governments to counteract the effects of the Dutch disease stemming from the massive exportation of raw materials that results from the exploitation of natural resources (Salama 2011).

As for commercial matters, China has signed three free trade agreements with countries in the region: Chile (2006), Peru (2010) and Costa Rica (2011). It is close to signing one with Colombia. Nearly ten years after the free trade agreement between Chile and China came into effect, exports from the former to the latter practically quadrupled, but their composition shows an increasing concentration of primary products (copper and its derivatives, iron ore, wood, fruits and other minerals; Svampa and Slipak 2018).

Likewise, the presence of capital of Chinese origin is increasingly important in the region. Some examples can be used to illustrate what has been said. In the hydrocarbons sector, four big companies of Chinese origin are present: Sinopec, the China National Petroleum Corporation, the China National Offshore Oil Company and Sinochem. By 2010 these companies were already participating in some fifteen extraction projects located in Peru, Venezuela, Ecuador, Colombia, Brazil and Argentina.

In terms of mining and metals, the main destination for Chinese investments has always been Peru, followed by Brazil and more recently by Ecuador. The most active firms are China Minmetals and Chinalco. In 2014, Minmetals bought from Glencore Xstrata the Peruvian mine of Las Bambas, one of the largest copper projects in the world. In Ecuador, the government of Rafael Correa granted concessions for the San Carlos, Panantza and Mirador copper mining projects to Ecuacorriente, which is owned by the Chinese public companies Tongling Nonferrous Metals Group and China Railway Construction Corporation. With these concessions, Chinese state companies control more than half of copper production and at least one-third of gold and silver production in Ecuador (Chicaiza 2014; Sacher 2016). In addition, it must be noted that in Argentina's province of San Juan, the Chinese firm Shandong Gold has acquired 50 percent of the gold-focused Veladero Project, responsible for two major cyanide spills (2015 and 2016) previous to its association with the Canadian company Barrick Gold.

Another more relevant issue is loans. Recent studies show that the majority of Chinese loans in the region have been for infrastructure (55 percent), followed by energy (27 percent) and mining (13 percent). The main lender has been the Development Bank of China, which has granted about 71 percent of all loans to the region, and the main beneficiary has been Venezuela, which has received slightly more than half of these funds to finance thirteen projects. As beneficiaries of the loans, Brazil and Argentina stand out, each having received close to 14 percent of Chinese loans made in the region. Chinese loans to Ecuador and Venezuela are taking the place of sovereign debt markets, are being guaranteed with oil or some raw material (loans conditioned by commodities) and include a requirement of Chinese company involvement in the project being funded.[1]

It is also worth examining the destination of investments from China. The findings of various studies align in showing that Chinese investments are established mainly in extractive activities (mining, oil, agribusiness, mega-dams), which reinforces the return to a primary economy brought about by the Commodities Consensus. In some Latin American countries, the economy has been oriented so that the tertiary sector supports the primary sector. This development threatens clusters of small and medium-sized companies, either due to environmental contamination or the possibility that raw materials that were previously processed by local small and medium-sized enterprises will instead be exported directly to China.

At the beginning of the Commodities Consensus and the rise of progressive governments, not a few analysts and politicians welcomed the emerging relationship between Latin American countries and China, arguing that it offered the possibility of expanding the region's autonomy in relation to US hegemony. Venezuelan president Hugo Chávez led this type of positioning, carrying out a notorious policy of rapprochement with China. Supported by oil wealth, Chávez saw China as a suitable commercial and political ally with which to distance himself from the United States. As the passage from a bipolar world to a multipolar one accelerated, the relationship with China became politically strategic in the geopolitical balance of the Latin American region. For the most optimistic, the new commercial linkage opened the possibility of a South-South collaboration between "developing" countries.

However, beyond China's label as an "emerging market" and the difficulty of accepting China's self-presentation as another developing country given its economic clout, it is clear that the Asian country's meteoric rise as well as the realpolitik of trade relations with Latin American countries are far from illustrating the vision of a symmetrical South-South relationship. As the progressive cycle advanced, the relationship between China and different Latin American countries attenuated the thesis of South-South cooperation. Likewise, the development of a defiant Latin American regionalism was tempered as a result of UNASUR's passage into a low-intensity period (Comini and Frenkel 2014), marked by the end of the strong regional leadership, including the deaths of Hugo Chávez and Néstor Kirchner, and the removal of Luiz Inácio Lula da Silva, three leaders who had strongly committed to regional integration.

A second question aims to evaluate the scope of Latin American regionalism. It must be remembered that one of the most important milestones of this new regionalism was the Mar del Plata summit, held in Argentina in 2005, when Latin American countries buried the possibility of the Free Trade Area of the Americas, which had been promoted by the United States. They created the Bolivarian Alternative for the Americas, instigated by the charismatic Chávez. In a clear Latin Americanist line, ambitious projects were planned, such as the creation of a single currency (sucre) and the Bank of the South, which, however, did not take off, in part due to declining enthusiasm on the part of Brazil, which was emerging as a powerful player on the world stage. The creation of UNASUR in 2007, and later the Community of Latin American and Caribbean States in 2010, initially as a forum outside of Washington through which to address conflicts in the region, characterized the regional integration process. However, all this was far from preventing bilateral free trade agreements between the United States and several Latin American countries, or the creation in 2011 of a new regional bloc, the Pacific Alliance, by Chile, Colombia, Peru and Mexico.

Both the thesis of a new defiant regionalism and that of South-South cooperation with China seem to have more to do with wishful thinking than with the actual economic and commercial practices of the different Latin American progressive governments. In fact, the signing of unilateral agreements with the Asian giant by Latin American governments (many of which commit their economies for decades) is far from being the exception. In recent times it is the general rule, and instead of strengthening Latin American integration, it enhances competition between commodity-exporting countries.

Although the irruption and rapid consolidation of the influence of the People's Republic of China in Latin America was seen as an opportunity to achieve greater autonomy from the United States, the resultant rhetorical Latin Americanism, unilateral negotiations with China, de facto competition between the different countries of the region, and increase in exports of raw materials ended up consolidating the asymmetries of the relationship and deepening the dependence on neoextractivism. Thus, the issue is not the linkage of the Latin American region to China but the way it operates through an unequal exchange and a demand for commodities. This relationship has translated into a promotion of extractivism and a re-emphasis on the primary sector of the economy in Latin America, in a context of declining regionalism.

The End of the Progressive Cycle as a Lingua Franca

The emergence of different progressive governments generated great political expectations among citizens. During the Commodities Consensus, progressivism became a sort of lingua franca — that is, a framework capable of not only unifying different political experiences through a common language but also ordering or ranking them, establishing a gradation from the more politically radical (the Bolivarian axis illustrated by Venezuela, Bolivia and Ecuador) to the more moderate (Brazil, Argentina, Uruguay and others). The modular elements that characterized this lingua franca were the questioning of neoliberalism, heterodox economic policies, the expansion of social spending and consumption and, finally, the aspiration to build a Latin American space, from which to think about regional integration. Undoubtedly, the consolidation of a progressive political hegemony associated with these modular elements was linked to the rise of international prices of raw materials, which in economic as well as political and social terms has been characterized here as the Commodities Consensus.

Throughout the progressive cycle (2000–15), there were those who tended to more or less automatically identify progressivism with leftism. However, at the national and regional levels, what was understood as progressivism was subject to harsh debates and interpretations, especially in relation to conceptions of social change, connections with social movements, the expansion of neoextractivism and other issues. This revealed the growing tension between different decolonizing political narratives, especially between the developmentalist narrative and the indigenist narrative, which played an important role in the period of change that started in 2000 — that is, in the questioning of neoliberal hegemony and the opening of a new political space. On one side, the developmentalist narrative, updated in terms of neoextractivism, merged with other dimensions typical of the populist tradition so deeply rooted in Latin America, while on the other side, the indigenist narrative, in keeping with the struggles against neoextractivism, merged with environmental and autonomist discourse and, towards the end of the cycle, with the discourse of popular feminism, marking the beginning of what I have termed the ecoterritorial turn.

However, it is important to take into account the gradations and nuances typical of each national context. In some countries, despite the consolidation of neoextractivism as a development strategy and the explosion of socioenvironmental conflicts, the dispute between different narratives did not occur with great intensity or have the same public visibility. Thus, in Brazil and Chile, the ecological narrative, with a focus on community, was associated with a set of hushed and scattered voices on the periphery of the periphery (Indigenous groups, peasants, assemblies of small and medium-sized towns), whereas in Bolivia and Ecuador, this narrative from Indigenous people and environmental organizations accrued a great amount of attention and relevance on the public agenda. Its association with concepts contained in the new political constitutions of Bolivia and Ecuador — such as *buen vivir,* plurinationalism and the rights of nature — granted those groups legitimacy, which would gradually be questioned by ascending populist movements.

This process of confrontation between the different political narratives was sharpened throughout the progressive cycle, amid not only the struggles against neoextractivism and the growing criminalization of socioenvironmental struggles but also the inadequacies and political and socioeconomic limitations of Latin American progressivism. Thus, the profuse language of rights, the reduction of poverty and policies of social inclusion and the increase of wages and consumption during the time of the fat cows of the Commodities Consensus would coexist with a strategy of forcing social organizations and movements into submission and intensifying the personalization of political power, along with a persistence of inequalities, an increasingly visible commitment to the extractive sectors, the notorious influence of transnational capital and rural transformation through an accelerated process of land-grabbing.

As the populist-developmentalist narrative was imposed as dominant and tendentially exclusive, absorbing and repurposing certain elements of other matrices (class-based and autonomist) and expelling those that were more annoying or difficult to incorporate (associated with the ecological and communitarian wings), the discussion about what was considered to be leftist sharpened. The fact is that towards the end of the progressive cycle (2015–16), political processes and recursive social dynamics through the decoupling of progressives and leftists became more pointed. In some cases, such as the Workers' Party in Brazil, a "genetic mutation" could be seen, as Modonesi (2016) points out; in others, the evolution was towards models of more traditional domination, anchored in a particular political tradition (forms of high-intensity populism; Svampa 2016); in both cases it was a "conservative modernization" (Schavelzon 2016; Singer 2013, among others).

Even the commitment to institutionalize a powerful Latin American space was cut short. Seen from a distance, a decade later, that 2005 Mar del Plata summit against the Free Trade Area of the Americas ended up becoming the high point of a defiant Latin American regionalism, when it should have been the starting point of a new integrationist Latin America, oriented towards the creation of a regional platform with the negotiating capacity to take on new and powerful commercial partners, among them China.

Outwardly, the progressives (populist or transformist) emphasized the ideological struggle with different groups of power, especially with big media. Along these lines, historically Latin American forms of populism in the twentieth century were associated with the social pact, even though it was attained through a language of war. The progressivism of the twenty-first century established a similar scheme — that is, on the one hand, they questioned neoliberalism, but on the other hand, they carried out the pact with big capital. Despite this, or precisely because of it, they soon found themselves immersed in a great political and ideological confrontation with sectors of the right, which allied with big media.

Thus, although in different ways and over different periods depending on the case, this polarization simplified the electoral competition, dividing the political field between two antagonistic blocs: the progressive forces, which claimed to represent the will of the people, and the various ascendant right-wing parties or coalitions supposedly rising to the defence of the republic. This simplification of the political space led to the exacerbation of conspiracy theories on the part of progressives: in the end it was the fault of the empire, of the omnipresent Right or of big media; moreover, from this point of view, any criticism of progressives (made by ecological, communitarian or Marxist leftists) ended up benefiting the Right. On the side of the Right-wing sectors, this opposition translated into the demonization of the different experiences under the progressive governments, which toward the middle and end of the cycle began to be characterized as "irresponsible populism,"[2] guilty of having wasted a period of prosperity associated with the boom of commodities and simply reduced to a matrix of pure corruption. For this, the right-wing sectors would also have their intellectuals, their salvific speeches and the support and promotion of big media.

The political overreaching of progressives, who at one point sought to establish the idea that they and only they embodied or could embody the will of the people, was fuelled by the growing economic crisis and corruption scandals. The increasing division and confrontation meant the mere possibility of electoral change was experienced, as an intense drama. This is the case in Venezuela, where the crisis is widespread and Maduro remains in power after being re-elected in May 2018 and despite being challenged by Juan Guaidó, the president of the National Assembly, in January 2019. It was in Argentina, in 2015, that the Right finally triumphed, and its power was consolidated two years later in the midterm elections. It also happened in Ecuador, in 2017, when Lenín Moreno established himself as the candidate of the Right to quickly distance himself from and break ties with his predecessor, Rafael Correa. The division and polarization was experienced even in the Bolivia of Evo Morales, one of the most successful presidents of the period. Among other things, he ignored a referendum in February 2016 that prevented him from running for president for a fourth consecutive time, and later a court ruled there would be no term limits, allowing him to stand for office again in the next election. Despite the overreactions, not everything is a conspiracy theory, as the processes of political polarization enabled several coups, as illustrated by the early expulsion of Manuel Zelaya in Honduras (2009), the rapid dismissal of Fernando Lugo in Paraguay (2012) and the impeachment of Dilma Roussef in Brazil (2016), which was aggravated later by the imprisonment of former president Luiz Inácio Lula da Silva (2018), all of which accelerated the return to an openly conservative situation in these countries.

The Limits of Existing Progressivism

The construction of progressive hegemony was associated with economic growth and poverty reduction. By 2012, the Economic Commission for Latin America and the Caribbean reported a fall in poverty (from 44 percent to 31.4 percent) as well as a decrease in extreme poverty (from 19.4 percent to 12.3 percent) from 2001 to 2011. This was due not only to the wage increase but also to the expansion of conditional cash transfer programs.

In line with the reduction of poverty, the first studies based on the Gini coefficient showed a reduction in inequality in different Latin American countries from 2002 to 2010. However, some years ago, several authors began to qualify such statements, maintaining that the available data only measured short periods and did not allow for a long-term view. Additionally, the drop in income inequality was tied to an increase in wages but not to a reform of the tax system, which became very complex, opaque and above all regressive (Salama 2015)

Other arguments introduce the distinction between structural and circumstantial inequality. While in the 1990s poverty and inequality increased in the region, in the first decade of 2000 both were reduced throughout the continent, which allows us to conclude that this trend is independent of the ideological leanings of governments and instead caused by structural economic factors linked to the region's position in the world system (Machado and Zibechi 2016). Further, the economic interests of the elites were not touched, as there was no tax reform. The tax system continues to be regressive; in 2013, the tax on the richest sectors provided 3.5 percent of total tax revenue, while the contribution of the value-added tax rose by one-third, providing 36 percent of total tax revenue, becoming the main source of tax collection in many countries (Burchardt 2016: 69).

Finally, more recent studies argue that the reduction of poverty in Latin America did not translate into a decrease in inequality. Research inspired by the work of Thomas Piketty, taking the tax declarations of the richest layers of the population, show that the top 1 percent of the income hierarchy in countries such as Argentina, Chile and Colombia appropriate 25 to 35 percent of national wealth (Kessler 2016: 26). Other research conducted in Brazil, one of the most unequal countries in the region, showed that the decrease of poverty from 2006 (the height of the commodities boom) to 2012 (the end of the boom) was not accompanied by a reduction of inequality in terms of income distribution and land ownership. Studies by the Institute for Applied Economic Research in this area have shown an increase in inequality since 2012, with the richest 1 percent appropriating 24.4 percent of the country's income (vs. 22.8 percent in 2006). As for the richest 10 percent, their share of national income over the same period increased from 51.1 percent to 53.8 percent (Zibechi 2015). Thus, although extreme poverty in Brazil and other countries in the "progressive" camp was reduced from 2002 to 2015, in many cases by 50 percent (lifting millions from the ranks of the poor and into the middle class as defined by its consumption capacity), inequalities persist and have even increased since the collapse of the commodities boom.

In short, the progressive governments made a pact with big capital (extractive and, in some cases, financial) outside the arena of electoral politics. Likewise, they made no or only timid reforms to the tax system, taking advantage of a period of extraordinary income collection. As Stefan Peters (2016: 22) points out, neoextractivism became a condition for the successful consolidation of progressive governments, but at the same time it was one of the major obstacles to the achievement of deep and structural reforms in the region.

Notwithstanding, the end of the progressive cycle does not mean the end of actually progressive governments. Uruguay and Bolivia, for example, remain on a progressive (neodevelopmental) policy path. Ecuador, however, like a number of other countries in the current context, was torn between a progressive mutation and a turn to the right in the 2017 election. As it turned out, with the betrayal of Correa's progressive project — the citizens' revolution — the new president Lenín Moreno allied with elements of the ruling class and turned sharply to the right, joining Argentina and Brazil, both of which in recent years have done the same and restored a neoliberal policy regime.[3] Meanwhile, the exception to the end of the progressive cycle is Mexico, after the triumph of Andrés López Obrador, even if it is necessary to say that it is a sort of progressivism out of cycle (or "late progressivism," as Massimo Modonesi, 2018, called it).The fact is that we are witnessing the end of progressivism as a lingua franca in the region. And this decline confronts us with a harsh reality: for the Left, the outlook is grim. The selective progressivism of so many Latin American governments in the context of a general rejection of neoliberalism ended up opening deep wounds that were difficult to heal within the space of electoral politics, as in the case of Ecuador, where sectors of the Confederation of Indigenous Nationalities of Ecuador, which in an earlier electoral cycle had identified with the Left, ended up voting for the candidate on the far right in the 2017 presidential elections.

The end of the progressive cycle is not something to celebrate. It encourages us to think about the dissociation between existing progressivism and Left progressivism, and about the evolution of these regimes towards more traditional models of domination: populism, transformations, passive revolutions. The new political cycle confronts us with a new scenario, increasingly devoid of a common language. Some progressive governments persist (with all their mutations), and there is even the possibility of adding other progressive experiences (Mexico). But the scenario also includes a restored Right, which exhibits an openly neocorporate language (Argentina and Brazil), especially after the triumph of Jair Bolsonaro in Brazil, which further suspends respect of freedoms and basic rights amid a deepening neoextractivism.

These continuities and ruptures occur in a framework that increasingly endangers the freedoms and basic rights of the most vulnerable populations. At the regional and global levels, this leads to a more atomized and unpredictable situation, which marks the end of the cycle of progressivism as a lingua franca and shows the advance of a regressive Right, which seeks to more openly promote the logic of capital in the territories.

NOTES

1. As of December 2014, Venezuela's public external debt to China amounted to approximately US$70 billion. Venezuela pays its external debt with 600,000 barrels of oil per day. In 2017, after a fall in production, Venezuela sent 330,000 barrels per day to China, according to the Center for Strategic and International Studies in Washington (Svampa and Slipak 2018).

2. The concept of populism has a long history and a negative political connotation. In Latin America, it is associated with nationalist or progressive governments, unlike what has happened in Europe and the United States. Certainly, both forms of populism in the mid-twentieth century and the twenty-first century were progressive, with limitations and deficits. Progressive populism is characterized by its ambivalence: on the one hand, it incorporates democratic elements and popular social majorities, and on the other hand, it deploys authoritarian elements, linked to concentration of power in the leader, fetishization of the state and a closing of channels of pluralism. Sectors of the right, especially on the political or media spectrum, tend to reduce this ambivalence to spoils for their followers, corruption and demagogy. I argue that this type of reading is partial and incomplete (Svampa 2016).

3. See Petras and Veltmeyer (2017) for more on this pendulum swing in electoral politics from centre-left progressivism to far-right neoliberal authoritarianism, and thus the end of the progressive cycle in Latin American politics.

REFERENCES

Burchardt, Has-Jürgen. 2016. "El neo-extractivismo en el siglo xxi: Qué podemos aprender del ciclo de desarrollo más reciente en América Latina." In Has-Jürgen Burchardt, Rafael Domínguez, Carlos Larrea and Stefan Peters (eds.), *Nada dura para siempre. Neoextractivismo despúes del boom de las materias primas*. Ecuador: Abya Yala.

Chicaiza, Gloria. 2014. *Mineras chinas en Ecuador: Nueva dependencia*. Quito: Agencia Ecologista de la Información.

Comini, N., and A. Frenkel. 2014. "Una Unasur de baja intensidad. Modelos en pugna y desaceleración del proceso de integración en América del Sur." *Revista Nueva Sociedad*, no. 250.

Kessler, G. (ed.). 2016. *La sociedad Argentina hoy: Radiografía de una nueva estructura*. Buenos Aires: Siglo xxi-OSDE.

Machado, Decio, and Raúl Zibechi. 2016. *Cambiar el mundo desde arriba. Los límites del progresismo*. Bogotá: Ediciones Desde Abajo.

Modonesi, Massimo. 2016. "Subalternización y revolución pasiva." In *El principio antagonista. Marxismo y acción política*. México: Itaca-UNAM.

Modonesi, Massimo. 2018. "México, el gobierno progresista tardío." *Nueva Sociedad*. <https://nuso.org/articulo/mexico-el-gobierno-progresista-tardio>.

Peters, Stefan. 2016. "Fin del ciclo: el neo-extractivismo en Suramérica frente a la caída de los precios de las materias primas. Un análisis desde una perspectiva de la teoría rentista." In Has-JuÀàrgen Burchardt, Rafael Domínguez, Carlos Larrea and Stefan Peters (eds.), *Nada dura para siempre. Neoextractivismo despús del boom de las materias primas.* Ecuador: Abya Yala.

Sacher, W. 2016. "Segunda contradicción del capitalismo y megaminería. Reflexiones teóricas y empíricas a partir del caso argentino." Doctoral dissertation. Flacso-Ecuador.

Salama, Pierre. 2011. "China-Brasil: industrialización y 'desindustrialización temprana.'" *Open Journal Sistem.* <http://www.revistas.unal.edu.co/index.php/ceconomia/article/view/35841/39710>.

Salama, Pierre. 2015. "¿Se redujo la desigualdad en América Latina? Notas sobre una ilusión." *Nueva sociedad.* <http://nuso.org>.

Schavelzon, Salvador. 2016. "La llegada de Temer: radicalización conservadora y fin de ciclo." September 9. <http://www.rebelion.org/noticia.php?id=217321>.

Singer, André. 2013. *Os sentidos do Lulismo: reforma gradual e pacto conservador.* São Paulo, Brazil: Cebrap.

Svampa, Maristella. 2016. *Debates Latinoamericanos.* Indianismo, Desarrollo, Dependencia y Populismo. Buenos Aires: Edhasa.

Svampa, Maristella, and A. Slipak. 2018. "Amérique latine entre vieilles et nouvelles dépendances: le rôle de la Chine dans la dispute (inter)hégémonique." *Hérodote,* 4, 171: 153–166.

Zibechi, R. 2015. "El mito del progresismo y la desigualdad en América Latina." URNG. <http://www.urng-maiz.org.gt/2015/11/el-mito-del-progresismo-y-la-desigualdad-en-america-latina/>.

6 Final Thoughts: Dimensions of a Systemic Crisis

Humanity is going through a systemic crisis of global reach, a crisis of civilization that includes different factors and is closely linked to the expansion of neoliberal capitalism.[1] Therefore, in this final chapter I provide a reflection on the different dimensions of the crisis, starting with the socioecological crisis and closing with the political crisis that Latin America is going through. To do this, I return to the concept of the Anthropocene, in order to establish its links with a critique of development and neoextractivism. I also advance some concepts that are needed to think critically about alternatives to the crisis.

Dimensions of the Crisis: The Anthropocene

The Anthropocene designates a new epoch in which human beings have become a force of transformation with global and geological scope. It replaces the Holocene, an epoch characterized by climatic stability, which lasted approximately ten thousand to twelve thousand years and allowed the expansion and domination of human beings on earth. The Anthropocene introduces the idea that we have reached a dangerous threshold that can lead to abrupt and irreversible changes as the result of global warming and its consequences, including mass extinction of different species and the consequent large-scale loss of biodiversity.

The term "Anthropocene" brings together two roots from the Greek: ἄνθρωπος (anthropos), meaning man, and καινός (kainos), meaning new or recent. It was proposed in 2000 by several eminent scientists, among them the chemist Paul Crutzen. The factors that justify talking about the passage to a new epoch are numerous. The first is global warming, resulting from the increase in emissions of carbon dioxide and other greenhouse gases. Currently, in relation to 1750, the atmosphere contains 150 percent more methane gas and 45 percent more carbon dioxide due to human-caused emissions. A consequence of this is that since the mid-twentieth century, the temperature has increased 0.8°C, and the Intergovernmental Panel on Climate Change foresees an increase of between 1.2 and 6°C by the end of the twenty-first century. Scientists consider 2°C to be the threshold after which increases become very dangerous. The overall increase in temperature could well be greater if everything continues as before (business as usual). The most recent systemic approaches and scientific advances show that even a slight variation in the average world temperature could trigger unpredictable and chaotic changes.

In 2017, the non-profit organization Carbon Disclosure Project released its *Carbon Majors Report*, finding that since 1988 more than half of global industrial emissions have come from twenty-five companies and state entities. Large oil companies such as ExxonMobil, Shell, BP and Chevron are among the biggest emitters. Also, according to said report, if fossil fuels continue to be extracted at the current rate over the next twenty-eight years, the average temperature rise will be close to 4°C by the end of the century.

The second critical factor is in regard to an anticipated loss of biodiversity — the destruction of the fabric of life and ecosystems. It is a recursive process; climate change accelerates the loss of biodiversity. In the last decades, the extinction rate of species has been a thousand times higher than the geological norm. That is why a sixth extinction is already being discussed, although unlike the previous five, which were explained by exogenous factors (global cooling or, in the case of the extinction of dinosaurs, the fall of an asteroid), the sixth extinction is of anthropic origin, which means human action is responsible for the destructive impacts to life on the planet.

Several years ago, in 2004, a group of scientists used the species-area relationship to calculate the risk of extinction in a context of climate change, using two extreme scenarios. In one estimation, if global warming were to remain at a low threshold, by 2050 between 22 percent and 31 percent of existing species would be condemned to extinction. But if global warming soared to a probable maximum, the percentage would rise to between 38 percent and 52 percent. Other studies have indicated different percentages (higher or lower), but the results are always alarming. Threatened species are many, from the solitary polar bear, which could disappear in a few decades if the ice sheets of the Arctic Ocean continue to be reduced, to the bees, whose colonies are suffering a collapse due to the use of pesticides, the appearance of various viruses and, of course, climate change.

It is not only terrestrial ecosystems that are threatened. The acidification of the oceans is another face of global warming, a product of the concentration of carbon dioxide, which changes the chemistry of water and endangers the life of marine ecosystems. Since the beginning of the Industrial Revolution, the average acidity has increased 30 percent due to the absorption of carbon dioxide from the burning of fossil fuels. It is estimated that the sea has absorbed some 500 billion tons of CO_2, "which is equivalent in weight to 500 billion Volkswagen Beetles thrown into the sea," according to Bonneuil and Fressoz (2013).

In a text full of ironies and sharp comments, American philosopher and feminist Donna Haraway (2016), citing the biologist Anna Tsing, argues that the Holocene was a long epoch in which there were still abundant areas of refuge, so that different organisms could survive unfavourable conditions and slowly repopulate. While successive waves of extinction have ended with a significant segment of species gone due to exogenous factors (climate change, major catastrophe), life on earth always showed a great capacity for resilience. The new and drastic change that the Anthropocene brings is the destruction of the space and the time needed for any organism, whether animals, plants or human beings, to find refuge and rebuild. All indications are that the acceleration of the process, in addition to its magnitude, hinders the very possibility of adaptation. Consequently, the Anthropocene is less a new age than a pivotal epoch, which forces us to recognize that what comes next will not be like what came before.

Another of the critical factors has to do with changes in biogeochemical cycles, which are fundamental for maintaining equilibrium in ecosystems. As happened with the carbon cycle, the cycles of water, nitrogen, oxygen and phosphorus, essential for the reproduction of life, passed into human hands in the last two centuries. The excessive increase in industrial activity, deforestation and soil contamination by fertilizers and water are altering these life cycles. For example, the growing demand for energy has led to the construction of dams and thus a change in the water cycle. "We dammed half our world's rivers at unprecedented rates of one per hour, and at unprecedented scales of over 45 000 dams more than four storeys high," according to Kader Asmal, chair of the World Commission on Dams, in a 2000 report. This has resulted in the displacement of millions of people. Besides the impact on ecosystems and the loss of natural goods and cultural heritage that have been submerged underwater, dams have displaced between forty and eighty million people worldwide. Some researchers consider this a conservative figure and believe it may actually be upwards of 100 million, of which the majority are Indigenous and peasant populations. The two most populous countries in the world, China and India, have the largest number of displaced people. In Latin America, Brazil leads with more than one million displaced people.

To this must be added the increase in the world population. The planet had 900 million human inhabitants in 1800 and now has almost 7.7 billion in 2019. The global ecological footprint of humanity today exceeds ecosystems' capacity for regeneration; it increased by 50 percent from 1970 to 1997. At present, humans consume one and a half times what the planet can provide in a sustainable manner. This means that the land needs more than a year and a half to regenerate what we have used and wasted in a year, a reality that places us on a path of unsustainability that will only get worse, because it is expected that by 2050 the world population will have grown to 10 billion people, most of them in emerging or developing countries. If the current consumption system persists, it is estimated that by 2030 we will need the equivalent of two planet earths to support humanity.

Another critical factor refers to changes in the consumption model, based on a scheme of planned obsolescence, which limits the useful life of products in order to force people to consume over and over again and to maximize the benefits to capital. This socioenvironmentally unsustainable practice, initiated by automotive companies, has been exacerbated since the 1960s by the industrial sector, which includes everything from household appliances, computers and cell phones to the textile industry. In turn, this process is part of a much more extensive movement linked to mutations of the food model that have occurred in the last decades. We have witnessed a significant turn towards a food model with enormous impacts on our health and on the lives of animals, plants and fields, promoted by state policies, the logic of the market and powerful business lobbies that operate behind society's back. Built by the large agri-food companies, this model leads to a degradation of all ecosystems, due to the expansion of monocultures such as soybeans and oil palms, which entail the annihilation of biodiversity; overfishing; contamination by fertilizers and pesticides; land clearing and deforestation; and land-grabbing. All these forms of production and ecological degradation are responsible for an increase in greenhouse gas emissions, not only during the production process but also in the transport of goods.

The Anthropocene, Criticism of Neoextractivism and Alternatives

The concept of the Anthropocene found footing in many areas. It expanded into not only the field of earth sciences but also social and human sciences, and even in the arts, becoming a point of convergence for geologists, ecologists, climatologists, historians, philosophers, and artists and art critics, among others.

For an important sector of scientists, including Paul Crutzen, the Industrial Revolution opened the new epoch — that is, the invention of the steam engine and the beginning of the exploitation of fossil fuels, first coal, then oil. This first phase was followed by a second one called the Great Acceleration, which began after 1945 and is illustrated by a large number of indicators of human activity ranging from societies' increasing dependence on fossil fuels, to the rising atmospheric concentration of carbon and methane, to the increased building of dams and passing through changes in the nitrogen and phosphorus cycles and the drastic loss of biodiversity. All these indicators show an exponential increase in anthropogenic impacts on the planet from 1950 onwards.

According to others, such as the Anthropocene Working Group, which is made up of a group of scientists at the University of Leicester and led by Jan Zalasiewicz, formerly of the British Geological Survey, the planet entered the Anthropocene a bit later. After seven years of work, at the end of 2016, this group of geologists completed stratigraphic tests showing traces of aluminum, concrete, plastic, the remains of nuclear tests, increased carbon dioxide, radioactive rain and other substances in the sediment. Consequently, this group asserts that the Anthropocene began in 1950, using as its marker the appearance of radioactive plutonium waste in sediments, resulting from the numerous tests of atomic bombs made in the middle of the twentieth century.

In contrast, for other analysts, such as Marxist historian Jason Moore, this is a long-term process, requiring an examination of the origins of capitalism and the expansion of mercantile borders in the long medieval period to account for the new epoch, which he prefers to call "capitalocene." The cycles of capital generated a historical-geographic model based on rapid appropriation of resources and geographic expansion and diversification once a resource was exhausted. "Is the soil exhausted? We move to the border. This was the motto shown on the coat of arms of early capitalism" (Moore 2013). Thus, the current crisis must be read as a long process in which new ways of ordering the relationship between humans and the rest of nature have taken shape.

From my perspective, it is necessary to demystify and stimulate the critical reach of the concept, to think of the Anthropocene in terms of the expansion of commercialization and the frontier, which forces us to return to the critique of neoliberal capitalism. This does not mean, however, that we have to abandon the concept of the Anthropocene. Rather, it is essential to stress the tension that runs through it, because it is a concept in dispute, crossed by different narratives, not all of which converge, not only with respect to when the new epoch began but, above all, what the possible exits out of the systemic crisis are. As a critical diagnosis, the Anthropocene challenges us to think about socioecological problems from another place. It establishes the idea that humanity has passed a threshold, bringing increasingly unpredictable, nonlinear and large-scale responses from nature. That said, it is evident that it is not just a crisis of humanity, of *anthropos*, understood in generic terms. To the extent that dominant economic and political actors continue to promote unsustainable development models, it is not only human life that is in danger but also that of other species and the planetary system as a whole, at least as we know it. Consequently, the Anthropocene necessitates the questioning of the current logics of development.

Through neoextractivism in the globalized periphery, the commercialization of all factors of production, linked to the current phase of neoliberal capitalism, is fully expressed, with the consequence of expanding the frontiers of capital accumulation through the large-scale imposition of unsustainable development models, combining extraordinary profits, destruction of territory and dispossession of rural populations. This is compounded by an increase in extreme events: fires, floods and droughts, which, in addition to being widespread, are linked to government policies that favour agribusiness and its food models, expansion of the oil frontier, mega-mining, mega-dams and others. In short, seen from the South, the association between the Anthropocene, the expansion of the commodity frontier and the exacerbation of neoextractivism is indisputable.

In the South, this has led to debate not only about the consequences of neoextractivism, which are impossible to hide, but also how to face the systemic crisis. To confront the socioecological and civilizational crisis posed by the Anthropocene entails thinking about alternatives to the dominant model of extractivism, of elaborating transitional strategies that mark the path towards a postextractive society. For this, it is necessary to overcome those hegemonic visions that continue to see development from a productivist perspective (indefinite growth), as if natural goods were inexhaustible, while conceiving of the human being as autonomous and outside or above nature. It also requires thinking about the transition and exit from the current pattern of development, something that encompasses not only neoextractivism in terms of the appropriation of nature and the model of accumulation but also the dominant circulation (of capital and investment) and consumption patterns.

The Anthropocene as a critical diagnosis requires rethinking the crisis from a systemic point of view. The environment cannot be reduced to one more expense column in a company's accounting, in the name of an alleged corporate social responsibility, nor to a policy of ecological modernization or a green economy, which points to the continuance of capitalism through the convergence of market logic and defence of new technologies proclaimed to be "clean." Finally, the current socioecological crisis cannot be seen as one aspect or another of the public agenda or even as another dimension of social struggles. It must be considered from a holistic, integral, decidedly inter- and transdisciplinary perspective.

From a theoretical point of view, and in line with the approaches of Alberto Acosta and Ulrich Brand (2017), it is possible to think about the transition through two concepts increasingly rooted in a global battlefield: postextractivism and degrowth. These two multidimensional concepts share different features or critical elements; for example, they provide a critical diagnosis of current capitalism, understanding it not only as an economic and cultural crisis but also, from a more global approach, as a socioecological crisis of civilization. Both make a critique based on the ecological limits of the planet while emphasizing the unsustainable nature of consumption and food patterns on a global scale, in both the North and in the South. Finally, these notions constitute the starting point for thinking about horizons of change and civilizational alternatives, based on an environmental rationality, different from the purely economic one that drives the process of commodification of life in its different aspects.

Indeed, in Latin America, the transition is thought about in new ways of inhabiting the territory, some of which are in the making, others in force, in the midst of struggles and social resistance that assume an anti-capitalist character. These new ways of living are accompanied by a political-environmental narrative, associated with concepts such as *buen vivir*, the rights of nature, common goods, postdevelopment, ethics of care and others. All these concepts are based on defence of the commons, which today is one of the keys in the search for a new emancipatory paradigm, in the confrontational discourse of social movements, both in the central countries, where defence of the commons is defined today by a struggle against the policies of adjustment and privatization (neoliberalism) and against the expansion of extreme energy, as in the peripheral countries, where it is defined above all as struggle against the different and multiple forms of developmental neoextractivism.

Certainly, in order to reverse the logic of infinite growth, it is necessary to explore and move towards other forms of social organization based on reciprocity and redistribution, which place important limitations on the logic of the market. From Latin America and from the Global South more broadly, many contributions have been made by the social and solidarity economy, youth, workers and peasants who believe the meaning of human labour is to produce use value or livelihoods. There is, thus, a plurality of experiences of self-organization and self-management by the popular sectors linked to the social economy, control of the production process and nonalienated forms of work, and others linked to the reproduction of social life and creation of new forms of community. For example, in a country associated with the soybean model, such as Argentina, there are networks of municipalities and communities that promote agroecology, proposing healthy food without agrotoxins, and lower costs and lower profitability, allowing more workers to be employed. A new agroecological framework is emerging, seeking to connect by bridges and footbridges an archipelago of experiences on the margins of the dominant soybean model, which is based on transgenic cultivation for export. Although they are modest, of a local and limited nature and always haunted by vulnerability and the possibility of co-optation, these experiences of self-organization are leaving their mark through the creation of a new social fabric, a range of possibilities and experiences that need to be explored and strengthened.

Over in Europe, the multiple dimensions of the crisis intersect with the questioning and failure of neoliberalism, visible in the exclusion of vast sectors from an increasingly exclusionary and unequal capitalist globalization, and in the normalization of a consumerist way of life, which promotes the acceleration of the social metabolism of capital (the demand for raw materials and energy). In the context of a crisis not only political and economic but also cultural, which reappeared in 2008, the idea of degrowth, launched in the seventies, has been given a kind of second life. Far from the literal understanding that some associate with the concept of degrowth (read simply as the denial of economic growth), the experiential lexicon developed in Europe in recent decades deepens the diagnosis of the systemic crisis (the limits of social, economic and environmental growth linked to the current capitalist model) and opens the imaginary of decolonization to a new social and political grammar, which highlights different proposals and alternatives: debt auditing, disobedience, eco-communities, urban horticulture, job-sharing, social currencies. For example, in an energy transition framework, transition towns — a pragmatic movement in favour of agroecology, permaculture, degrowth, consumption of locally or collectively produced goods and recovery of life skills and harmony with nature — are being promoted. Born in Ireland in 2006, this movement aims to create a caring culture, crowd-source solutions to community challenges and use clean and renewable energies, with a strong increase in energy efficiency. Communities in transition seek to generate social resilience against the progressive social collapse caused by climate change, the depletion of fossil fuels and the deterioration of political regimes.

Relational Approaches and Pathways of Interdependence

The anthropocenic turn has deep philosophical, ethical and political repercussions; it forces us to reconsider ourselves as *anthropos*, but also, in a central way, it leads us to rethink the link between society and nature, between humans and non-humans. For a century now we have abandoned the organicist vision of nature — Gaia, Gea or Pachamama — that our ancestors professed. As children of modernity or offspring colonized by it, we have related to nature through an anthropocentric and androcentric episteme, whose persistence and repetition, far from leading us to a solution to the crisis, has become an important part of the problem.

In its most critical versions, the anthropocenic turn poses a questioning of the cultural paradigm of modernity, which is based on an instrumentalist vision of nature as useful to the expansionist logic of capital. The anthropology and critical philosophy of the last decades has insistently reminded us of the existence of other ways of relating to nature, of viewing the link between humans and non-humans. In other words, not all cultures or historical times, even in the West, developed a dualistic approach to nature. Not all peoples travelled the same path, isolating nature or considering it a separate, external environment at the service of human beings. There are other matrices of a relational or generative type, based on a more dynamic vision, as happens in some Eastern cultures, where the concept of movement, of becoming, is seen as the principle that governs the world and is embodied in nature, or those immanentist visions of American Indigenous Peoples who conceive of human beings as part of nature, immersed in it and not separate from or in opposition to it.

These relational approaches, which emphasize the interdependence of life and different forms of relationship between living beings, between humans and non-humans, take different names: animism, for the anthropologist Philippe Descola, and Amazonian or Amerindian perspectivism, for Eduardo Viveiros de Castro. Thus, for Descola (2011), while the naturalism (dualism of society and nature) associated with Western culture is based on the idea that humans share the same physical reality as animals (corporeity) but are differentiated by their interiority, in animism all beings have a similar interiority but are differentiated by their bodies. For his part, Viveiros de Castro makes a similar argument in his well-known essay *La mirada del jaguar*, where he conceptualizes the Amazonian relation to nature. Amerindian perspectivism affirms that the world is populated by many species of beings endowed with conscience and culture, and each of these beings sees itself as human and others as non-human, like animals or kinds of spirits. In contrast to the dominant vision today, the common ground between human and non-human is not animalism, but humanity. Humanity is not the exception, but the rule; each species sees itself as human and, therefore, as a person, possesses and (re)creates a kind of culture. "Humanity is the universal basis of the cosmos. Everything is human" (Viveiros de Castro 2008).

These different relationships with nature question the constitutive dualisms of modernity. In this line, the Colombian writer Arturo Escobar argues "that anthropologists, geographers and political ecologists have shown with increasing eloquence that many rural communities in the Third World 'construct' nature in ways strikingly different from the dominant modern forms: they identify, and thereby use, natural environments in very particular ways. Ethnographic studies of Third World scenarios show a number of significantly different practices of thinking, relating, constructing and experiencing the biological and the natural" (Escobar 2000: 71).

These "relational ontologies," as Escobar (2011, 2014) calls them following anthropologist Mario Blaser, make the territory and its communal logics a condition of possibility.[2] The interrelation generates spaces of synergy between the world of humans and the other worlds that surround the world of humans. These spaces materialize in practices, manifest as mountains and lakes, and are understood to have life or be living spaces, which of course is difficult to demonstrate from the European positivist position (Escobar 2011, 2014).

In addition, when rethinking our link with nature from a relational perspective, the ethics of care and ecofeminism undoubtedly open up other possible ways. Their contributions can help us to rework the links between the human and the non-human, to question the reductionist vision that comes from the ideas of autonomy and individualism. Certainly, the ethics of care offers another gateway in the necessary task of rethinking our link with nature by placing at the centre the notion of interdependence, which, in the current civilizational crisis, should be read as ecodependence. The universalization of the ethics of care, as Carol Gilligan (2015) affirms, opens up a process of greater liberation, not only feminist liberation but the liberation of all humanity.

This line of action is reflected in the increasing involvement of women in the struggles against neoextractivism and its different modalities. These struggles open up a dynamic that questions the dualist view consolidated by Western modernity, which considers nature as something external, liable to be dominated and exploited. At this crucial point, forms of popular feminism are weaving a different relationship between society and nature through the affirmation of the notion of interdependence, in which the human being is understood as a part of nature, within it, as a result promoting an understanding of human reality through recognition of others and nature.

The leading role that women in Latin America are assuming in the struggles against the expansion of the extractive frontier and land-grabbing is a paradigmatic illustration of this double process. Listening carefully to their individual and collective voices makes it possible to see a strong identification with the land and its vital cycles of reproduction, as well as a demystification of the myth of development and the construction of a different relationship with nature. Not infrequently, the demand for a free, honest voice— "our own voice" — is emerging that questions patriarchy in all its dimensions and seeks to relocate care in a central and liberating place, undeniably associated with the human condition. Thus, in an increasingly commodified world, where the totality of our natural commons is increasingly subject to the pressure of neoliberal capitalism, the ethic of care becomes a cornerstone for rethinking gender relations, as well as relationships with nature.

Thus, these struggles have been affirming other ways of talking about the valuation of a territory, other ways of building a link with nature and other narratives about Mother Earth, which re-create a relational paradigm based on reciprocity, complementarity and care, pointing to other modes of appropriation and dialogue of knowledge, to other ways of organizing social life. These new languages are nourished by different politico-ideological matrices, from anti-capitalist, ecologist and indigenist to feminist and anti-patriarchal perspectives, which come from the heterogeneous world of the subaltern classes and cross the human and social sciences, earth sciences and even the realm of avant-garde art. These languages constructed from below constitute the essential starting points in the process of building another conviviality, other ways of inhabiting the earth. In short, relational approaches that take on a new significance in the systemic crisis tell us that we live in a world in which ontological plurality is based on the multiplicity of worlds — "pluriverses" as Escobar maintains —which entails respect for other ways of understanding culture and organizing life.

Dimensions of the Crisis in Latin America

Up until a few years ago, Latin America was considered to be moving in the opposite direction of a global process marked by increasing social inequalities. However, towards the end of the so-called commodities supercycle, social and economic indicators showed a worrying panorama after more than ten years of growth and expanded consumption. Certainly, Latin American governments — especially the progressive ones — increased public social spending, managed to reduce poverty through social policies and improved the situation of lower-income sectors, based on a policy of increased wages and consumption. However, they did not reduce inequality. By not touching the interests of the most powerful sectors, by not making progressive tax reforms, as explained in the previous chapter, inequalities persisted in the midst of economic concentration and land-grabbing.

Thus, from a longer-term view, the expansion of neoextractivism translated into a series of disadvantages, which undermined the idea of comparative advantages that some were able to defend during the time of the fat cows of the Commodities Consensus. Neoextractivism did not lead to a jump into manufacturing, instead refocusing economies on the primary sector, which was aggravated by the entry of China as an unequal partner in the region. At the same time, the dropping prices of raw materials generated a trade deficit that led governments to take on more indebtedness and extractive projects and thus enter a perverse spiral, which cemented their role as dependent exporters of primary products and increased violations of human rights.

The link between neoextractivism, land-grabbing and inequality is evident. Latin America is not only the most unequal region on the planet, it also has the most unequal distribution of land as a result of the advance of monocultures and dispossession, to the benefit of large companies and private landowners. Neoextractivism has produced profound impacts in rural areas because of monocultures, which have reshaped land disputes with poor and vulnerable populations. Thus, the expansion of the agricultural frontier was done in favour of the major economic actors, who are interested in implementing transgenic crops such as soybeans, oil palms, sugar cane and others. The data from the agricultural censuses of fifteen countries show that "in the region as a whole, the largest one percent of farms concentrate more than half of agricultural land. In other words, one percent of farms occupy more land than the remaining 99 percent" (Oxfam 2016).

Finally, beyond their internal differences, the prevailing development models share a common logic, entailing large-scale and intensive occupations of land, the amplification of environmental and sociohealth impacts, the pre-eminence of large corporate actors, low-intensity democracy and violations of human rights. In this line, we must remember that Latin America has another sad ranking, because it is the region where the most human rights defenders and environmental activists are assassinated, a sinister indicator that has worsened in the last ten years during the expansion of the extractive frontier and the criminalization of socioenvironmental protests. The opening of a new cycle of human rights violations underscores the limitations of the democratic governance models in the region, and even more so the retraction of rights. This involves the violation of basic political rights, the right to information, the right to demonstrate and the right to participate in collective decisions (consultations, referendums), as well as the violation of land and environmental rights found in the new constitutions and in national and international legislation.

This undeniable reality, which eats away at democracy and tears away at the social fabric of Latin America, has erected new walls between competing narratives across the region, especially between, on the one hand, populist and developmentalist progressivism, with its statist vision and its tendency towards concentration and personalization of political power, and on the other hand, the radical political language developed by Indigenous and social movements along with the emergence of a new socioenvironmental agenda. In short, the passage from the Washington Consensus to the Commodities Consensus brought problems and paradoxes that dampened the rebellious nature of social movements and limited the horizon of Latin American critical thinking, engendering theoretical and political ruptures that crystallized in a bundle of ideological positions that were difficult to process and resolve. Further, the current exacerbation of extractive dynamics, with their extreme forms, enhances the different dimensions of the crisis. Unlike previous periods, where the environmental dimension was just one part of struggles and not addressed explicitly, the current ecoterritorial struggles in Latin America reveal a new understanding of the problem in a social, territorial, political and civilizational sense, questioning the hegemonic vision of development and therefore the dynamics of neoliberal capitalism.

Thus, it becomes necessary to investigate those collective experiences that are nourished by values such as reciprocity, complementarity, social and environmental justice, care and harmony in relations of interdependence between humans and non-humans. In Latin America there is an ecoterritorial perspective, which is proactive and emphasizes agroecology; there is an Indigenous perspective, which emphasizes community, decolonization and *buen vivir*; and an ecofeminist perspective, which emphasizes the ethics of care and dismantlement of the patriarchy. These approaches and languages seek the decommodification of common goods and the development of viable alternatives based on local and regional economies, experiences of agroecology, community spaces (peasant and Indigenous) and more.

To close, we should remember this: as the questioning of neoliberalism ushered in a new era, Indigenous Peoples led the struggle and the development of an emancipatory language (*buen vivir*, the rights of nature, autonomy, plurinational state), but the end of the progressive cycle and the beginning of the next era has been marked by the struggles of women, at different intensities and levels, against (though not exclusively) neoextractivism. In other words, Latin America moved from the "Indigenous moment" to the "feminist moment," adding the ecofeminist language of the body/land, the ethics of care and the affirmation of interdependence to the narrative of *buen vivir* and the rights of nature. Thus, the narrative of decolonization, associated with the Indigenous moment, now also includes the demand for dismantlement of the patriarchy ecodependence, linked to the feminist moment.

In sum, in a global ideological context where the rights of corporations predominate and xenophobia is ascendant, and in a region where the Left is in crisis and politics have taken a conservative turn, the task of rethinking and re-creating critical anti-systemic thinking emerges as a great challenge. Bridges must be built between genuinely leftist sectors, starting with the inclusion of the diagnosis of the global crisis, which is connected to the appropriation and exploitation of nature promoted by neoliberal capitalism and closely linked to neoextractivism. Without this, there is no possibility of reforming the political and intellectual space of the Left. Put simply, in both Latin America and in other places, if the Left is to (re)build, it will have to be not only popular, pluralistic and decidedly antipatriarchal but also deeply ecological.

NOTES

1. Along this line I agree with the perspective offered by the book *Alternativas Sistémicas*, published in 2017 by the Solón Foundation (Bolivia), Attac France (France) and Focus on the Global South. The book establishes a diagnosis in terms of a "systemic crisis" regarding the global workings of the capitalist system, and takes a tour of different concepts in critical development studies, such as *buen vivir*, the rights of nature, ecofeminism, the commons and deglobalization.

2. In different latitudes, they gave rise to a profuse anthropological literature on the ontological turn. See Holbraad and Pedersen (2017).

REFERENCES

Acosta, Alberto, and Ulrich Brand. 2017. *Salidas del laberinto capitalista. Decrecimiento y Postextractivismo*. Madrid: Icaria. <https://www.rosalux.org.ec/pdfs/Libro-Salidas-del-Laberinto.pdf>.

Bonneuil, Christophe, and J. Baptiste Fressoz. 2013. *L'événement antrhopocène: La terre, l'histoire et nous*. París: Le Seuil.

Carbon Disclosure Project. 2017. *The Carbon Majors Database: CDP Carbon Majors Report 2017*. <https://6fefcbb86e61af1b2fc4-c70d8ead6ced550b4d987d7c03fcdd1d.ssl.cf3.rackcdn.com/cms/reports/documents/000/002/327/original/Carbon-Majors-Report-2017.pdf>.

Descola, Philipe. 2011. "Más allá de la naturaleza y la cultura." In Leonardo Montenegro (ed.), *Cultura y Naturaleza, Aproximaciones a propósito del Bicentenario de Colombia*. Bogotá: Jardín Botánico de Bogotá José Celestino Mutis.

Escobar, Arturo. 2000. "El lugar de la naturaleza y la naturaleza del lugar: ¿globalización o postdesarrollo?" In Edgardo Lander (ed.), *La colonialidad del saber: Eurocentrismo y ciencias sociales. Perspectivas latinoamericanas*. Buenos Aires: Consejo Latinoamericano de Ciencias Sociales. <http://biblioteca.clacso.edu.ar/clacso/sur-sur/20100708045100/7_escobar.pdf>.

Escobar, Arturo. 2011. "Cultura y diferencia: La ontología política del campo de cultura y desarrollo." *Revista de investigación en Cultura y Desarrollo*. <http://biblioteca.hegoa.ehu.es/system/ebooks/19420/original/Cultura_y_diferencia.pdf?1366975231>.

Escobar, Arturo. 2014. *Sentipensar con la tierra: Nueve lecturas sobre desarrollo, territorio y diferencia*. Colombia: Ediciones Unaula.

Gilligan, Carol. 2015. *La ética del cuidado*. Barcelona: Cuadernos de la Fundación Víctor Grífols i Lucas. <http://www.secpal.com/%5cdocumentos%5cblog%5cCcuaderno30.pdf>.

Haraway, Donna. 2016. "Antropoceno, Capitaloceno, Plantacionoceno, Chthuluceno: generando relaciones de parentesco." Revista Latinoamericana de Estudios Críticos Animales.

Holbraad, Martin, and Morten Axel Pedersen. 2017. *The Ontological Turn: An Anthropological Exposition*. Cambridge University Press.

Moore, J.W. 2013. "El auge de la ecología-mundo capitalista (ii): las fronteras mercantiles en el auge y decadencia de la apropiación máxima." *Filosofía, política y economía en el Laberinto*, 39: 21–30.

Oxfam. 2016. "Unearthed, Land, Power and Inequality in Latin America." <https://www.oxfam.org/sites/www.oxfam.org/files/file_attachments/bp-land-power-inequality-latin-america-301116-en.pdf>.

Solón, Pablo, comp. 2017. *Alternativas Sistémicas*. La Paz: Fundación Solón-Attac France-Focus on the Global South.

Viveiros de Castro, Eduardo. 2008. *La mirada del jaguar. Introducción al perspectivismo amerindio (entrevistas)*. Buenos Aires: Editorial Tinta Limón.

World Commission on Dams. 2000. *Dams and Development: A New Framework for Decision-Making*. <https://www.internationalrivers.org/sites/default/files/attached-files/world_commission_on_dams_final_report.pdf>.

Index